BACK FROM CAPTIVITY

Rebuilding Your Identity in Christ

JENNIFER JOHNSON

randall house

114 Bush Rd | Nashville, TN 37217
randallhouse.com

© 2011 by Jennifer Johnson

Published by Randall House Publications
114 Bush Road
Nashville, TN 37217

All rights reserved. No part of this publication may be reproduced, stored in a retrieval system, or transmitted in any form or by any means—electronic, mechanical, photocopy, recording, or any other means—except for brief quotation in critical reviews, without the prior permission of the publisher.

All Scripture quotations, unless otherwise indicated, are taken from The HOLY BIBLE, NEW INTERNATIONAL VERSION®. NIV®. Copyright© 1973, 1978, 1984, 2010 by International Bible Society. Used by permission of Zondervan. All rights reserved. Other Scripture quotations are from Amplified Bible (AMP) Copyright © 1954, 1958, 1962, 1964, 1965, 1987 by The Lockman Foundation. Used by permission. All rights reserved.

Printed in the United States of America

ISBN 9780892656202

Dedicated to my husband—
thank you for holding on to the One who holds us.

Table of Contents

Introduction

At that time I will gather you; at that time I will bring you home. I will give you honor and praise among all the peoples of the earth when I restore your fortunes before your very eyes (Zephaniah 3:20)

Does your spiritual life resemble a car crash survivor who has temporarily lost the use of his legs? Did you take a few wrong turns somewhere, even though you thought you were on the road that led to satisfaction? Did your car spin out of control, and the only thing you knew to do was cry out to Jesus? You miraculously survived the wreck, but are unable to pull yourself out of the wreckage without Divine rescue. Immediately, you are rushed to the emergency room. This is no time for the family doctor, only a specialist will do. After a complete evaluation, you are in need of some intensive care. You desire things to be the same as they were before you left that dreadful day headed for what you thought would be freedom and happiness. Realizing the accident was no "accident," this event will forever change you. You look down at your limp legs and see that you must learn to walk again.

Let's evaluate your present spiritual condition: Do you need to learn to walk again? Is your life in jeopardy? Good news! There is a road to recovery. Walking again on your own will require hard work, but you are not alone in this journey to wholeness. With God as your Healer and with encouraging friends, you will discover what freedom and happiness truly are. Don't worry about your little strength; it will be just enough to begin the journey toward a renewed and intimate relationship with your Rescuer and Deliverer, Jesus Christ.

As the Israelites, God's chosen people rebuilt their identity after returning to Jerusalem from captivity, so we can learn from them in our own experience. "I will bring Judah and Israel back from captivity and will rebuild them as they were before." (Jeremiah 33:7). *Back From Captivity* is a guide to strengthen the foundation and walls of your intimacy with God as well as give you eyes to see your future from God's perspective. This Bible study is divided into three parts. First, we will focus on the present—getting through one day at a time. Second, we will glimpse back into the past— where you were before you had your "accident." Third, we will peer into your future.

This Bible study is written for those who call themselves a "Christian," not only in word, but also by how they once lived. They are members of a church and read their Bibles regularly, participated in church activities, and may have even held a leadership position. From someone else's perspective this person is a "Christian." Yes, this person genuinely asked Jesus into his or her heart, was baptized, and lived the Christian life as best he or she knew how. But, this person began to make some wrong choices or just simply stopped believing God and ended up somewhere he or she thought he or she would never be. But by the grace of God, today, this person is seeking Him again and wondering how to restore and rebuild his or her relationship with Jesus Christ. As I reference "leaving home" and "coming home," I don't necessarily mean a physical departure. To "leave home" refers to the departure from an intimate relationship with God and to temporarily follow primarily after the desires of your flesh. To "come home" simply refers to a decision to leave the path of destruction and to begin again following Christ and His ways with a desire to deepen your relationship with Him.

Hop in. Buckle up. Stay awake. This time from the passenger's seat. I'll drive; I've been down this road before. This will be one ride you will never regret.

Ah, Sovereign LORD, you have made the heavens and the earth by your great power and outstretched arm. Nothing is too hard for you (Jeremiah 32:17).

PART 1
PRESENT

Day 1 — Desolate Waste

Today's Scripture:

This is what the Lord says: "You say about this place, "It is a desolate waste, without people or animals."

—Jeremiah 33:10

Welcome. I greet you today with a huge smile and warmth in my heart. Just the thought of you opening your Bible and beginning a study of God's Word is nothing more than living proof that God is *your* God. To think of where you've just come from and the fact that you humbly open the Bible means something has changed in your thinking. It truly means you have matured. It means you made the decision to turn to God for direction, hope, love, and answers to life's questions because you now know that without Him, you have no real, meaningful life. I want to tell you, "Congratulations!" Maybe no one has said that to you, especially in your present circumstances, but I truly congratulate you on your decision to come home and to actually turn to God for divine help. Returning home may have been one of the hardest decisions you have ever made and quite possibly ever make. No one can "make you" return home; that was your decision. Praise God!

Throughout this study, we will compare our lives with the prodigal in Luke 15 and with the Israelites as they returned home to Jerusalem after being in Babylonian captivity for 70 years. In reference to the Scriptures pertaining to the Babylonian captivity (exile), Ralph W. Klein states, "In these writings, we will see that the depths of the Exile were the occasion for some of the most profound insights in the entire Old Testament. These writers made the most of a disaster." (Ralph W. Klein, *Israel in Exile*, Philadelphia: Fortress Press, 1979, *p. 7*).

I believe God has much to reveal to us about Himself and ourselves through His written Word, which is amazingly so relevant to us today. The enemy can still take us captive into our own exiles. While in captivity we may have reflected on our life before we left home, but didn't know how to get it back, nor did we know if we even wanted it again. We remembered what we had and even longed for it, but it seemed so far from reality because captivity quickly took on a life of its own. *Back From Captivity* will aid you in putting the pieces of your life back together.

 Please marvel at the words of Romans 15:4 and write in your own words why it is applicable for us to read the Old and New Testament.

Understanding that participating in a Bible study is a giant-step in the recovery process of being home again, please take your time as you complete each day's study. This week's study will focus on who we are— how we see ourselves and how God sees us.

Please read Jeremiah 33:10. God described the land of Jerusalem where the temple once stood after it had been completely destroyed by fire when the Babylonians captured Judah. Jerusalem was the place God's people, the Israelites, came to worship Him. It was in the temple that God would manifest His presence and accept their offerings. When the Israelites were allowed to return home to Jerusalem, they came back to nothing but rubble. The place that had once meant so much to them was now in ruins.

The word *desolate* in the Hebrew language is *chareb,* which means "to parch (through drought)."

Maybe that is just how you have been feeling lately—dry, spiritually dry. I believe that without daily "living water" (John 7:37-38) one of the consequences is emptiness.

The prodigal son also experienced emptiness at his lowest point and said to himself, "and here I am starving to death" (Luke 15:17).

 Describe how you may be feeling in terms of being desolate.

I distinctly remember a worship service I attended a few months after I was home from captivity where the speaker began his message with a lengthy prayer. At that moment, I had never felt more spiritually empty. So many wonderful, rich words were overflowing from his heart for all our ears to hear. I remembered that I too had once been able to pray aloud in a group with words that came from deep within my spirit. But at that moment, if someone had asked me to pray aloud, I felt like I had absolutely nothing to offer.

 Now read with great hope the promising words of God in Jeremiah 33:10-11. What is God personally saying to you in these verses?

God promises that He "will restore the fortunes of the land as they were before." The "fortunes" for us are the spiritual wealth of peace, joy, and love that will overflow out of the depths of our spirit and onto the lives of those around us. The emptiness we feel on the inside will be full of rich treasures, which are not based on circumstances but on God's beautiful presence in our lives. Although man sees rubble, God sees treasures. You may feel like you are no good anymore, like nothing good could ever come from you, but in Christ you are in an amazing position for God to perform miracles.

"The city will be rebuilt on her ruins, and the palace will stand in its proper place. From them will come songs of thanksgiving and the sound of rejoicing" (Jeremiah 30:18b-19a).

Let's pray:

Dear heavenly Father, may the sound of joy and gladness quickly come from my mouth as You do miracles in me. I give thanks to You, Lord Almighty, for You are good and Your love endures forever. In Jesus' name I pray, Amen.

Week 1 — Who Am I?

Day 2 — Worthy

Today's Scripture:

I am no longer worthy to be called your son; make me like one of your hired servants.

—Luke 15:19

Through the course of this study, one thing I pray we will not only discuss, but actually accomplish is how to make decisions based on what we know to be true rather than the way we feel. We will not neglect our feelings because they are very real and strong, but we will learn to understand the necessity of not living according to how we feel. I think it is fair to assume that each one of us has made a wrong decision based on the way we were feeling at the moment. At the time it seemed appropriate, but afterward we may have actually felt worse. For instance, we may feel like not forgiving someone because we think he or she doesn't deserve it. As time goes by, the bitterness and anger in us over the situation builds up, and we become easily angered towards other people who wrong us. It is vital we see the importance of knowing what the truth is, especially when it directly affects our emotions and actions. Beth Moore in *When Godly People Do Ungodly Things* wrote, "Your injured heart will be protected by your *doing* what is right until you *feel* what is right." (Beth Moore, *When Godly People Do Ungodly Things,* Nashville: Broadman and Holman Publishers, 2002, p. 208.)

From the list below check off the questions you have recently asked yourself.

❍ Who am I?

❍ Does God love me?

❍ Does God care?

❍ Am I worthless?

❍ Can I go to church?

❍ Do I belong back home?

❍ How do I get back to
   where I used to be?

❍ Am I a Christian?

❍ Does God want me?

❍ Can God still use me?

❍ Will I go to heaven?

❍ What do others think of me?

❍ Have I messed up too much?

❍ Can I stay home?

 What are some other related questions you have asked yourself?

These are all good questions. Although the questions may cause you to feel like you are not worthy of being called a Christian, the questions in themselves are worth an answer. The answers will come from our heavenly Father's words.

The Israelites who had been taken captive by the Babylonians for 70 years and returned to their homeland in Jerusalem must have had numerous questions as to who they were as individuals and as a nation. Their former identity as God's people in the Promised Land given to them by God as promised to the Patriarch Abraham (Genesis 15:7) was certainly put to the test. There was no Davidic king on the throne, no temple to worship God, and no wall for protection. As scattered Israelites made their way into Jerusalem, they must have wondered if they could make it again amidst the destruction of their former home.

First and Second Chronicles were two of the last books written in the Old Testament and were written to the Israelites after their return home from captivity. Glance through First Chronicles 1—8. What is recorded?

In their search for identity, the chronicler started with the beginning of time to prove through the genealogy that they were still God's people. "It begins with Adam and follows his genealogical descent through Abraham to Jacob and Esau. Its purpose is to define the place of God's chosen people in world history." (Charles F. Pfeiffer, *Wycliffe Bible Commentary,*Chicago: Moody Press,1990, p.369)

 How does the retelling of the genealogy of Israel's history speak to you in your search for identity?

 Fill in the blanks to 1 Chronicles 9:2. "Now the first to resettle on their _____ property in their _____ towns were some Israelites, priests, Levites and temple servants."

They belonged there. The land was still theirs. God in His abounding grace validated them: "So you will be my people, and I will be your God" (Jeremiah 30:22).

In the parable of the lost son recorded in Luke 15:11-31, the son questioned his identity. After living in sin, then "coming to his senses" and wanting to go home, he did not even perceive himself as being a legitimate son of his father. He only saw himself as hired help. The son made the right decision to go home, but his feelings were not correct in the way he felt about his identity.

Please read Luke 15:17-24.

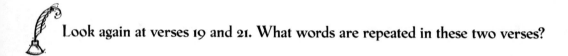 Look again at verses 19 and 21. What words are repeated in these two verses?

Now look at verses 20 and 22. Notice the word *but* that follows the statements in verses 19 and 21. The son, the legitimate son, felt all he was destined to be was hired help, BUT the father had much, much higher plans for his own son. You see, the son's feelings were incredibly strong, but the truth was that his feelings were not the truth.

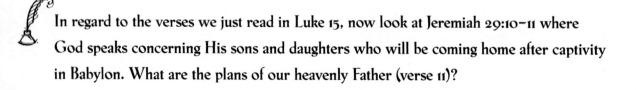 In regard to the verses we just read in Luke 15, now look at Jeremiah 29:10-11 where God speaks concerning His sons and daughters who will be coming home after captivity in Babylon. What are the plans of our heavenly Father (verse 11)?

In Jeremiah 29:10 God says, "I will come to you." In Luke 15:20, we read "he ran to his son."

Describe your moment of being in your heavenly Father's arms again for the first time after you decided to come back to Him. Did you "see" Him coming to you?

We may feel hopeless, worthless, inadequate, dirty, unusable . . . BUT GOD . . .

BUT GOD . . . . You fill in the blank. What is God saying personally to you today through His Word?

Let's pray:

Turn those thoughts into a prayer to your Father who has plans for you that "no eye has seen, no ear has heard, no mind has conceived what God has prepared for those who love him" (1 Corinthians 2:9), and write your prayer in the space below.

Week 1 — Who Am I?

Day 3 — Every Branch

This week's study is centered on who we are at this particular time as we have made the grand decision to return to the Lord and live according to His desires for our lives. Today we will catch a unique glimpse of who we are.

Many times in the Bible God compares people to trees. One such example is a dream God gave to King Nebuchadnezzar of Babylon. King Nebuchadnezzar needed Daniel, a Hebrew captive, to interpret the dream for him. Before we get to the dream and its interpretations, let's read a few verses in the New Testament. Please read John 15:1-5 and answer the following questions:

Today's Scripture:

He cuts off every branch in me that bears no fruit, while every branch that does bear fruit he prunes so that it will be even more fruitful.

—John 15:2

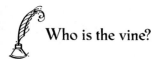 Who is the vine?

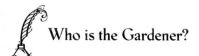 Who is the Gardener?

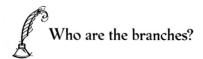 Who are the branches?

13

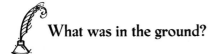 What does the Gardener do to every branch that does not bear fruit?

I pray that through the reading of these Scriptures, you were affirmed once again that you are a child of our heavenly Father—that you are His, and you belong to Him. God, as the Gardener, will only cut off the branches of those who are His children. This time in your life may be painful, but child, it is not in vain!

What is the promise in verse 5?

If you feel anything like I did when I first came home again, you may feel more like a bulldozer had run over you than just a few branches being trimmed. With that in mind, let's look at the dream Daniel interpreted for King Nebuchadnezzar, who was also the king that God allowed to take the Israelites from Jerusalem and into captivity. Daniel lived in Babylon before, during, and after the attack on Jerusalem.

Turn to Daniel 4:23 and read what Daniel replied to the king as he retold the king's dream.

What was left of the tree?

What was in the ground?

The tree, representing King Nebuchadnezzar (Daniel 4:20-22), had once been beautiful, strong, fruitful, sheltering, and great, but now the Lord was going to allow it to be cut down with only the stump and roots left.

The fact that you are alive today and actually participating in a Bible study is proof that you are at least a "stump." I am convinced you have some roots deep in you affecting your decision to return to the Lord. These roots are part of your spiritual heritage. Roots include:

- ❍ Family members who have prayed for you since you were born
- ❍ Daily quiet times between the Lord and you
- ❍ Attending church services
- ❍ Answered prayers
- ❍ Intimate moments where you felt the Lord's presence
- ❍ Going to youth camps/retreats
- ❍ Asking Jesus in your heart
- ❍ Being baptized
- ❍ Participating in a small accountability group
- ❍ Singing in a choir
- ❍ Family members who are Christians

 Put a check mark beside the ones that pertain to you.

The difficult part to read in Daniel 4:23 was about the tree being cut and destroyed, was it not? The fact of the matter is that as a child of God, sometimes He needs to cut off parts of us because those parts are not a reflection of Him. "Beloved, sometimes a prolonged rebellion and resisted warning can result in drastic chastisement, but God's desire, particularly toward His beloved child, is neither to destroy or condemn. It is to regrow us free of the fruit-rotting parasite of pride. God is not trying to destroy us. He is trying to keep us from destroying ourselves."(Beth Moore, *Daniel*, Nashville: LifeWay Press, 2006, , p 84.)

Please read the last interpretation of the dream as described in Daniel 4:26.

 What was the condition on which King Nebuchadnezzar's kingdom would be restored?

He was to acknowledge that something much bigger and greater than he ruled. You see, King Nebuchadnezzar had attributed the greatness of Babylon to himself (Daniel 4:30); when in fact, it was God who had given him prosperity (Daniel 2:37-38). It was his pride that led God to "cut down the tree" in his life.

 When was the moment you realized it was time to acknowledge that Someone other than yourself should be ruling you?

In the book, *The Prodigal Comes Home,* Michael English, a contemporary Christian artist, said about himself, "The most amazing thing is that God rerouted me without condemnation. Yes, I still had regrets—many of them. But after I reset my life's compass toward Him, it didn't matter that the other roads in life were straighter or that they would have gotten me there faster. What mattered was that finally—finally—after years of wallowing with the pigs, I had come home."(Michael English, *The Prodigal Comes Home,* Nashville:Thomas Nelson, 2007, p.199.)

Let's pray:

Dear heavenly Father, I acknowledge today that You are the Ruler of my life. I choose today to follow and obey You wholeheartedly. Thank You, Father, that You have much fruit for me to bear that will bring You glory and honor. I bless you, Jesus. In Jesus' name I pray, Amen.

Week 1   Who Am I?

Day 4 — Hopeful

In the Introduction, I compared someone who was a survivor of a car wreck to someone who took some wrong turns spiritually, but is now learning how to live again inside God's will for his or her life. I need you to understand that just as someone who gets hurt physically and needs a doctor and special treatment in the intensive care unit, so you too, are in the spiritual intensive care unit and in need of the Specialist. Your spiritual heart has been bleeding for quite some time; it needs some healing.

To put it in sports terminology—you are benched. You are on the sidelines of the game getting yourself stronger so that when you are put in the game again, you will be an effective team player. You are obviously not dead and you are not off the team, just temporarily sidelined. This is definitely not time to sit around, mope, and have a pity party. Lots of work will be required of you if you truly desire to "walk again" or "play the game."

Today's Scripture:

Yet this I call to mind and therefore I have hope.

—Lamentations 3:21

 You will not do this work alone. In the space below, please write and believe in your heart God's words in Zechariah 10:12.

I wholeheartedly believe God will undoubtedly use His Word, the Bible, as one of the main sources for your healing. I believe this to be true because of the tender, sweet healing I received from my heavenly Father when I chose to spend time alone with Him through reading my Bible. Another reason I believe His Word to be healing is simply because God says it is.

 **Write Hebrews 4:12.**

The word *powerful* can also be interpreted as *active* (NASB), which is a medical term meaning it is effective and engaged in work. His word is a medicine that heals as deep as our wounds. Psalm 107 is a psalm believed to have been written by a Levite in celebration of God's goodness to the Israelites in their return home from the Babylonian captivity.

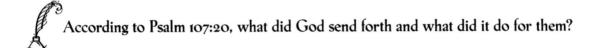 **According to Psalm 107:20, what did God send forth and what did it do for them?**

No matter how much trouble and heartache we've had, and no matter the day, time, season, or year "The grass withers and the flowers fall, but the word of our God endures forever" (Isaiah 40:8). Can I get an Amen?

The Old Testament book of Lamentations is written from an eye-witness perspective of the destruction of Jerusalem in 586 B.C. when King Nebuchadnezzar ordered the Babylonians to destroy the city and to either kill or take captive the Israelites. Jeremiah was one of the few who escaped both the killing and captivity, but fled to another city. Jeremiah is credited with writing Lamentations, although the book is anonymous.

Yesterday we discussed the importance of understanding our feelings in light of the truth. Today's reading will echo the same importance. Please read aloud the words of Lamentations 3:17-26. At what point (verse) does the writer switch his thoughts from what he is feeling to what he knows to be the truth?

 Write the verse that divides the feelings part from the truth of the matter.

 In verses 17–20, the writer is contemplating his present emotional state because of his remembrance of his past. When you are alone and stop to think about where you were when you were away from home, what do you feel?

Maybe you could sum up the way you feel into one word—miserable. Maybe you would even say "haunted." The writer says, "I well remember them" (verse 20) meaning he can remember his past afflictions with all the details like it was yesterday. Let's take special note of what the writer does immediately when his thoughts begin to affect his soul. Verse 21 is the turning point of when the writer's feelings shift to thoughts on what he knows to be true.

 Specifically, what does his mind recall in verses 22–23?

Even to you, dear child, even to you, God's compassions are new to you every morning. Great is God's faithfulness to bestow compassion on you every morning!

I must say an aloud "Hallelujah" as the writer talks to himself in verse 24 about His God. Write what he says.

The word *portion* in the Hebrew means *inheritance*. Child, say that aloud: "The Lord is my inheritance!" What do those powerful, medicine-like words mean to you?

Luke 15:14 says that the prodigal had "spent everything." So, he *thought* he had spent all of his inheritance on "wild living" (Luke 15:13), but his Father had an inheritance stored up for him that could not be spent. In 2 Corinthians 1:20, God tells us that all His promises come true for us through the person of Jesus Christ. Ephesians 1:3 identifies our inheritance, "Praise be to the God and Father of our Lord Jesus Christ, who has blessed us in the heavenly realms with every spiritual blessing in Christ."

Although we may deserve to live in misery, we have hope in the truth of God's Holy Word. God chooses instead to bless us every morning with His unfailing compassions. We have hope!

Let's pray:

Dear heavenly Father, others may see me and say that I am hopeless, but that is a lie. In You, Jesus I have every spiritual blessing. "Let the morning bring me word of your unfailing love, for I have put my trust in you. Show me the way I should go, for to you I lift up my soul" (Psalm 143:8). In Jesus' name I pray, Amen.

Day 5 — You Died

What a great week it's been studying the Scriptures with you. I hope you have felt 'full' as you completed each day's study. I hope your "legs" look a little less limp and that taking a walk/jog around the block doesn't seem so far out of reach anymore (spiritually speaking, of course). It is just fine if you need to do each day's study in more than one literal day. I am grateful you desire God's Word and are taking steps in the right direction. May God never be able to say of us again, "They went backward and not forward" (Jeremiah 7:24b).

Let's get started on today's study as we conclude our week focused on "Who am I?"

I am not going to ease into this truth. As a believer in Jesus Christ with the Holy Spirit living inside of you—YOU ARE DEAD. That's right—DEAD. You, as yourself, are dead. Colossians 3:3 states this difficult and mysterious truth, "For you died, and your life is now hidden with Christ in God." Now fill in the blank with your name then say it aloud.

> **Today's Scripture:**
>
> *For you died, and your life is now hidden with Christ in God.*
>
> —Colossians 3:3

For _____ died, and my life is now hidden with Christ in God. (Colossians 3:3)

What does this truth say to you in this exact moment? Please write your thoughts about what it means and feels like for you to know that *you are dead* (speaking in the sense of your sin nature).

We as believers don't just want to casually skim over this powerful verse and put all the emphasis on the "hidden with Christ" segment. Before we can successfully appreciate our lives with Christ on this side of heaven, I believe we need to successfully grasp death to self. Romans 6:6-7 clarifies and supports Paul's words in Colossians.

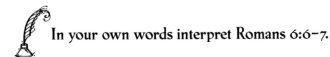 In your own words interpret Romans 6:6-7.

The Amplified Bible enables us to understand more fully the direct meaning of the two verses. It reads, "We know that our old self was nailed to the cross with Him in order that [our] body [which is the instrument] of sin might be made ineffective *and* inactive for evil, that we might no longer be the slaves of sin. For when a man dies, he is freed (loosed, delivered) from [the power of] sin [among men].

Underline/Highlight the phrase that describes why our old self was nailed to the cross with Christ.

I will never forget the moment a pastor, who was counseling and praying with me in the course of my return home, spoke these words over me, "Jennifer's dead." I wanted to scream and cry. The reality of my selfish desires meaning nothing struck me intensely.

I realized that even though my words had portrayed that God was in control of my life, my heart's motivations wanted what Jennifer wanted, and not God's will.

At that particular time in my life, I absolutely loved Rick Warren's book *The Purpose Driven Life*, especially the first words, "It's not about you." I got that logically. But, emotionally I would cry out, "But what *about* me?" "What about *me*?" I desperately wanted my needs met. I suppose it goes as far back as the Garden of Eden when Eve chose her needs over what God commanded (Genesis 3:6).

 Please write Galatians 2:20 in the space below and consider memorizing.

 What part of that verse jumps out at you? In other words, which words seem to have been written just for you and what do you think God is saying specifically to you?

I am reminded of Corrie ten Boom. Her book, *The Hiding Place*, is one of the best testimonies of God's forgiveness and mercy. My very favorite line in the book is when she is in the concentration camp trembling as she reads from her smuggled New Testament Bible. She writes, "I marveled sometimes that the ink was dry."(Corrie Ten Boom, *The Hiding Place* ,Old Tappan:fleming H. Revell Co.,1971, p. 195.). God's Word is timeless.

Living "dead," also referred to as "the crucified life," may be new to you as it was to me. It is going to take practice to live this new kind of living. Having lived "dead" for a little while now, I can honestly say that God's living is much greater than any living I could ever dream of.

In *The NIV Application Commentary* David Garland sums up Colossians 3:3 this way, "Since Christ is not one of the serving angels but reigns overall, all of our lives should be ruled by him. Every thought, aim, value, aspiration, and striving should come under his lordship." (David Garland, *The NIV Application Commentary: Colossians and Philemon,* Grand Rapids: Zondervan, 1998, p. 202.)

In 1 Corinthians 15:31, Paul says, "I die everyday—I mean that, brothers."

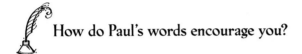 How do Paul's words encourage you?

I am convinced that this is how the martyrs of God (persons who were killed because of their belief in God), including Paul, could die without denying God. They had already died. Their life was no longer theirs; it was wholly God's. They died everyday. Physical death would only mean that now they could leave this earth and live in heaven with the One who died for them.

God wants us to die to ourselves so that we can truly live in Him, through Him, for Him, and with Him. It's bold. It's radical. It's abundant. Never think for one second you are missing out on something because you have chosen to live "dead." To not live "dead" would mean you've missed your very reason to be alive.

As we move forward to next week's focus—"What Do I Do?"—inhale the very words of Titus 2:14. "Who gave himself for us to redeem us from all wickedness and to purify for himself a people that are his very own, eager to do what is good."

Let's pray:
Dear heavenly Father, I choose today _____ *to die to myself and to live my life hidden in you. Amen.*
                                                    (date)

Week 2 — What Do I Do?

Day 1 — Turn to the Lord

Some Christians have a powerful testimony concerning their lives before they met Christ, of how much sin they were involved in, and of how far they were from a righteous life. When they asked Jesus into their heart, their lives were never the same. This Christian can remember being drawn to and lost in many destructive ways, and can even remember how God rescued and saved him from sin. He never wants to live the life he once did because of finding an abundant, new life in Christ.

My testimony, like many others, is not like that. My testimony is of one who accepted Jesus Christ as a little girl (of which I am deeply thankful), but then in my adult years (when I knew better) acted like a lost person and participated in destructive ways as a saved princess of the King. I relate to the prodigal in Luke 15 because I too left my Father's house in search of earthly/worldly happiness. I also relate to the Old Testament Israelites who were warned many times what God would do if they, as God's chosen people, continued in rebellion.

Sometimes it is difficult to associate the terms *fool*, *wicked*, or *evil man* with a Christian. We tend only to characterize non-Christians as fools, wicked, and evil. Unfortunately even Christians can act foolishly, do wicked things, and think as an evil person. In the Proverbs, Solomon emphatically conveys to his son the importance of listening

Today's Scripture:

Let the wicked forsake his way and the evil man his thoughts. Let him turn to the LORD, and he will have mercy on him, and to our God, for he will freely pardon.

—Isaiah 55:7

to him and not forsaking his teachings (Proverbs 1:8; 2:1; 3:1, 4:1; 5:1; 6:20; 7:1). Solomon wanted his son to know that unless you intentionally follow God and His ways, you can be easily drawn to what is evil resulting in harm. Proverbs 8:35-36 says, "For whoever finds me finds life and receives favor from the LORD. But whoever fails to find me harms himself; all who hate me love death."

 So, what do we do when we come to our senses and realize we have acted more like a fool than a son or daughter of the King?

 Please read the Father's words in Revelation 2:4-5. Write the two things God says to do.

1.

2.

 Take a moment and remember one of the greatest, most intimate moments you had with your Father before you left home? What does that memory say about your relationship with God?

I am so grateful we can still remember our previous intimacy with our Father. Our memories are of Him—it *was* Him in those memories. We didn't conjure up a story or incident; those memories were real God encounters. He's been so good to us! And you know what, child? He isn't finished! He has BIG plans for you!

The Amplified Bible version of Revelation 2:5 reads, "Remember then from what heights you have fallen. Repent (change the inner man to meet God's will) and do the works you did previously [when first you knew the Lord]."

In the early stages of being back from captivity, your natural tendency could still be to desire what you just repented from. To wake-up each morning and decide you are no longer going to pursue what you want, but instead do what God desires will require complete determination and obedience. The more you make a conscious effort to practice this kind of living, the easier it becomes, and the more you realize that God's will is actually better than yours! Your future holds freedom from what held you captive.

 Now is the time to do what you used to do when you walked with the Lord and knew His intimacy and goodness. Think about the things you did that promoted dialogue, enhanced peace, initiated worship, and produced joy. Did you sing praise songs? Did you go to church? Did you talk with Christian friends? Did you read your Bible? Did you go to retreats, camps, or conferences? Did you pray before a meal or before bedtime? Did you fast? Write down all the things you remember participating in that encouraged your relationship with your Heavenly Father.

Before we conclude today, I want you to see one more passage of Scripture. Please read Matthew 7:24-27. What is the difference between the wise man and the foolish man?

A true born-again believer can either be foolish or wise. When you participate in a Bible study, go to church, or go to a Christian camp, it isn't the participation that makes you wise, successful and strong; it is when you "put them into practice". You become a wise person when you *do* what you *heard* God told you to do.

Let's pray:

Dear Heavenly Father, You have been so good to me. You have been with me all along. Forgive me for not recognizing You. I want to be wise. I want to do what You want me to do. Help me, Jesus. I choose to set my life on You, my Rock. Amen.

Week 2 | What Do I Do?

Day 2 — Repentance

I am not sure exactly where you are right now on this journey of healing and wholeness, but one thing for sure is that I want you to stay on this path and be confident that you are on the right one. When a physical therapist wants to strengthen the muscles of an injured leg, we want him to work only on the injured leg. The physical therapist knows the appropriate exercises to perform for complete healing and range of motion, but if the exercises are performed on the wrong leg, it doesn't do the injured leg any good. Godly sorrow and repentance are a must on this journey. We need to be sure that we have the right kind of sorrow—*godly* sorrow and not *worldly* sorrow.

The word "sorrow" in the Greek means "sadness, grief, grievous". Do you remember the moment you began grieving over your wandering away from a close relationship with your Heavenly Father? If sin was involved, do you remember the first time you felt sad because of what you had done? In the space below describe your feelings as well as the circumstances at the time your grief/sadness began.

In Jeremiah 31:19, Ephraim testifies, "After I strayed, I repented; after I came to understand, I beat my breast. I was ashamed and humiliated because I bore the disgrace of my youth."

To make sense of our sorrow it is important to understand the context in which it occurred. If our sorrow was brought on because we

Today's Scripture:

Godly sorrow brings repentance that leads to salvation and leaves no regret, but worldly sorrow brings death.

—2 Corinthians 7:10

were caught, then we need to make sure we were not just sorry we got caught and experienced painful consequences. Instead we must be truly sorrowful about the sin. If our sorrow was brought on by a strong conviction in our conscience that we are not where we should be, and that we need to make changes, then we are on the right path. Along with sorrow, we may have experienced guilt and remorse because we began to realize the hurt we have caused ourselves as well as others. If your sorrow has led you to go a different direction toward godliness, then you are on the road of repentance.

The Lord said He heard Ephraim's moaning and his request for restoration. The Lord replied to Ephraim, "Is not Ephraim my dear son, the child in whom I delight? Though I often spoke against him, I still remember him. Therefore my heart yearns for him; I have great compassion for him."(Jeremiah 31:20).

I believe God's heart yearns for me and for you. He continues to love and show us mercy. He desires a close relationship again. How can we possibly refuse?

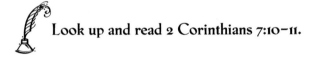 Look up and read 2 Corinthians 7:10-11.

According to verse 10 would a person who has godly sorrow regret repenting? Have you regretted repenting? If so, why? If not, why?

Beth Moore states in *When Godly People Do Ungodly Things*, "Tragically, inauthentic repentance is exactly what has given Christian restoration a bad name. If we're still able to strut around like an arrogant rooster, something's wrong. That's not repentance. But when true repentance comes (feeling more like a dead duck), God will not hesitate for a moment to forgive, cast the sins in the sea of forgetfulness, and put the child on the road to restoration."(Beth Moore, *When Godly People Do Ungodly Things,* Nashville:Broadman and Holman Publishers, 2002, p. 210.)

 From 2 Corinthians 7:11 list the results godly sorrow produces in the repentant person.

Having godly sorrow and a repentant heart, you will understand the seriousness of your condition/situation, the necessity of confessing your wrong-doing to those involved, the depth of anger toward yourself, the fear of consequences, the longing for restoration, the concern for the feelings of others, and the desire for justice.

Having worldly sorrow means that your guilt has kept you away from God, you lie to yourself by saying you don't need God or anyone else, you blame others, you become indifferent to your sin, you continue to meet your own needs, and you are consumed with yourself with no regard to your spirituality.

 Which type of sorrow do you possess? From the above lists of the 2 types of sorrow, what do you relate to the most?

Let's pray:

For our prayer today, let's pray a portion of David's prayer in Psalm 51. Dear Heavenly Father, "Create in me a pure heart, O God, and renew a steadfast spirit within me. Restore to me the joy of your salvation and grant me a willing spirit, to sustain me."(Psalm 51:10, 12)

Week 2 — What Do I Do?

Day 3 — Who Survived

Off and on in my life I have written in journals. I am particularly grateful for the times I wrote in a journal regarding my life back from captivity. At the time I wrote in it to help me keep my thoughts straight; it was a release for me. The moments I had with God were extremely personal and intimate. You see, when I wrote in my journal I was basically writing my prayers out to God. I told Him everything — all my feelings and emotions even if they were not pretty. My life was messy at the time and I knew He could help.

The book, *A Parable About The King*, by Beth Moore is a sweet story about a girl who was the daughter of a king and lived in a palace. She decided she didn't want to be royal anymore but wanted instead to be like a village peasant girl, so she ran away. She disguised herself and joined the crowd in the town and played games with the other children. Soon she realized she was too different and that she truly belonged in the palace. She fearfully went back home not knowing what the king would do or say or even if he would let her back in. Much to her surprise, the king welcomed her home and called her his princess. Then, "That night, after he had dressed her wounds, he tucked her into her soft bed and kissed her goodnight. He had even helped her to clean the mess she had left in her

Today's Scripture:

They said to me, "Those who survived the exile and are back in the province are in great trouble and disgrace. The wall of Jerusalem is broken down, and its gates have been burned with fire."

—Nehemiah 1:3

room."(Beth Moore, *A Parable About the King,* Nashville:Broadman and Holman Publishers, 2003, p. 26.)

When you look at your life at this very moment, do you see a "mess"? I will share with you something I journaled: "I guess I haven't realized until lately how sick I've been- spiritually. It seems the depth is catching up to me. It seems the more I dig myself (with God and some close friends) out of this pit, the more I realize how deep I had gone." As I began taking an inventory of where I was spiritually, I realized the mess I had allowed myself to get into. What does your "mess" look like? Don't worry about *how* you got into the mess- there will be plenty of time for considering that.

 For now, just write down some areas in your life that resemble a "mess".

I understand the humiliation and embarrassment associated with the messes, but if you haven't actually written exactly what your messes are in the above question, please do so. Sometimes it helps to see it in black and white. Now, something else I really want you to do if you haven't already. I want you to tell someone about your messes. I am convinced God wants to show up in your life through someone who can help. Let me show you through Scripture.

 Look at Today's Scripture Nehemiah 1:3 and write the messes that were told to Nehemiah about the current condition of Nehemiah's hometown of Jerusalem.

I would like to explain the term "Nehemiah" by describing what to look for in someone. Something like – A "Nehemiah" is someone who you can trust to tell them where you are spiritually. This person loves you and can see beyond your disastrous ways to see you how God sees you. He/she will pray for you, over you, and with you. He/she will have the understanding to know when and how to rebuke you in love as well as admonish you in your good choices.

Nehemiah 1:4 says that after hearing of Jerusalem's messes Nehemiah wept, fasted, and prayed for many days. At this particular time, Nehemiah was the cupbearer to the King Artaxerxes. He prayed and asked God to give him favor in the king's eyes to let him go and help his people. "And because the gracious hand of my God was upon me, the king granted my requests. So I went to the governors of Trans-Euphrates and gave them the king's letters. The king had also sent army officers and cavalry with me."(Nehemiah 2:8b-9). Child, HELP IS ON THE WAY. The surviving exiles in "great trouble and disgrace" had an army and cavalry on the way and they had yet to know of it. Know, it dear child, God's army and cavalry are coming to your aid. Let someone see your rubble and receive help.

After spending time examining the ruins, Nehemiah approached the surviving exiles and said: "'You see the trouble we are in: Jerusalem lies in ruins, and its gates have been burned with fire. Come, let us rebuild the wall of Jerusalem, and we will no longer be in disgrace.'"(Nehemiah 2:17).

 Write what the people replied in Nehemiah 2:18b.

And the rebuilding began.

Pray for God to send a "Nehemiah" your way. It will be alright for him/her to see your "trouble" and "disgrace"; he/she wants to help. If

God has already sent you a "Nehemiah" please don't hide anything from this person. The more you bring to light the darkness, the quicker your recovery and restoration. God has sent this person to you as a source of knowledge, comfort, guidance, and love. Embrace the help. "Two are better than one, because they have a good return for their work." (Ecclesiastes 4:9).

Let's pray:

Dear Heavenly Father, You see my rubble. My sin is not hidden from You. Lord, send a "Nehemiah" my way for help. I wave a white flag of surrender knowing I cannot rebuild myself and that an outsider can see things in me I cannot. Thank you, Jesus. Thank you. In Jesus' name I pray, Amen.

Week 2 | What Do I Do?

Day 4 — Greater Glory

Today's Scripture:

"The glory of this present house will be greater than the glory of the former house," says the LORD *Almighty.*

—Haggai 2:9

Henry Blackaby in his popular book, *Experiencing God,* states, "You will never be able to develop a Christ like character on your own. Despite your best efforts, and all the self-help books you might read only Christ can produce a Christ like character. This is accomplished as the Holy Spirit works in your life." (Henry Blackaby, *Experiencing God,* Nashville: LifeWay, 1990, p.48.). In this process of rebuilding, a "Christ like character" is really what we are pursuing is it not? Our integrity has taken a beating and we now need to rebuild what is left of it.

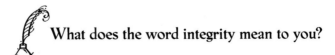 Take a moment to reflect on how you define a Christ like character, then write your thoughts.

What does the word integrity mean to you?

In your particular situation, you may be the only person directly hurt because of your past lack of integrity, or you may have hurt a whole string of people. No matter how much damage has occurred- your integrity and Christ like character can be rebuilt. I believe on the basis of Scripture that it will not only be rebuilt, but that it will manifest (visibly produce) greater glory for God than if the damage had never occurred. Wow! That was a bold statement. Read it again. Before you start to disagree with me, let's see what God has to say! Fill in the blanks to the following Scriptures (which all happen to be in context of the Israelites who survived the Babylonian exile and captivity and are back home in Jerusalem):

Zephaniah 3:19b "I will give them _____ and _____ in every land where they were put to shame".

Haggai 2:9 "'The glory of this _____ house will be _____ than the glory of the former house', says the LORD Almighty."

Jeremiah 33:9 "'Then this city will bring me _____, _____, _____, and honor before all the nations on earth that hear of all the _____ things _____ do for it; and they will be in _____ and tremble at the _____ _____ and peace I provide for it.'"

Isaiah 61:7 "instead of their _____ my people will receive a _____ _____, and instead of disgrace they will _____ in their _____; and so they will inherit a _____ _____ in their land, and everlasting _____ will be theirs."

These blessed promises of God are for us as we seek Him with our whole heart. As the Israelites were left with physical ruins, God promised peace and prosperity in their city. As we perceive ourselves as having little strength and hope, God promises He will cause good things in us that will cause others to see the difference in us and give God glory.

What if when the Israelites returned to Jerusalem found that someone had done an "Extreme Makeover- Temple Edition"? What if the rubble was gone? Would they have remembered their sins that led them to the captivity? Would they have remembered God's grace in bringing them home again? What are your thoughts?

I don't want to forget where I have been because then I may be prone to forget what God has done for me.

Let's go back to the book of Haggai and read the context of Today's Scripture. Please read Haggai 2:1-5. How many times does God declare to "be strong" in verse 4?

God declared to Zerubbabel (the man appointed to rebuild the temple), the high priest, and all the people to be strong. Then the Lord added "and work". He comforted the people by telling them He is with them and that His Spirit is among them.

Child, you have work to do. This work will require the knowledge that you are not alone and the comfort that God still resides in you through the gift of the Holy Spirit. What is this "work"? Right now, it may be in the little things such as: getting out of bed, choosing to have a good attitude, eating, or going to work/class. It may be that you need to do what you know is right even though you feel like going back to the old patterns or thoughts. It may be in asking someone for forgiveness. It may be to separate yourself from an individual or group. It may be to stop isolating yourself and to participate with family and friends.

In the space below, write what you feel the Holy Spirit is leading you to do.

An amazing picture of having to do work that requires strength but not feeling adequate for the task is in the movie *Facing the Giants*. If you have seen the movie- remember with me (If you haven't – go rent it tonight!). In the movie, during football practice the team is on the side of the field where the coach is encouraging them to be a better team as they anticipate a tough game that Friday night. The coach singles out one player, Brock, to stand up and get on the field where the coach blindfolds him. He tells Brock to get on his hands and feet. The coach then tells another player to get on Brock's back. Brock is now instructed to do the "death crawl" across the field with one of his teammates on his back. The coach is right beside him all the way telling him he can do it and to "give me your best". As Brock crawls down the field in tears, he tells the coach, "It hurts". The coach tells Brock, "I know it hurts" as he gets down on his hands and knees face- to- face with Brock encouraging him to keep going. Finally, after much sweat and tears the coach takes off Brock's blindfold and shows him he is in the end zone. Brock went the whole length of the football field carrying a teammate doing the "death crawl" using every bit of strength he didn't even know he possessed. Brock could not have done that without the encouragement of his coach.

Child, keep the faith. Don't quit. I know this will be a difficult time for you and emotionally exhausting. There will be days when you wonder if you are going to make it. On those days feel the presence of your Father down on the field encouraging you. God says in Hosea 11:4, "I led them with cords of human kindness, with ties of love; I lifted the yoke from their neck and bent down to feed them." Please know that there is an "end zone" in sight where there will be rest! Philippians 4:13 will never be more applicable than now, "I can do everything through Him who gives me strength." Your Heavenly Coach will never leave your side. He believes in you, and you are needed for the team.

Let's pray:

Dear Heavenly Father, You have good things planned for me as I put my hope, trust, and very life in Your hands. Reveal to me the work You desire me to do in Your name. I look forward to others seeing You in me. Amen.

Week 2 — What Do I Do?

Day 5 — Undivided Heart

We've learned many things this week to strengthen our relationship with our Heavenly Father. Day 1 we learned to remember our past relationship with God and to begin again doing spiritual disciplines that rekindle our love for Him.

Today's Scripture:

Teach me your way,
O LORD, and I will walk
in your truth; give me an
undivided heart, that I
may fear your name.

—Psalm 86:11

 Have you been doing that? If so, what have you done lately that you haven't done since before you left home? Write what you did and your feelings about it.

 Day 2 we identified the difference between godly sorrow and worldly sorrow. Do you have godly sorrow? What evidences of godly sorrow have you noticed?

If you long for godly sorrow be patient with yourself; this is a process. You can't force it, but you certainly can ask God to give you godly sorrow – He'll answer that prayer!

Day 3 we realized we have some messes "in our room", and we are in need of someone's guidance to help us clean up. Our "compass" is all over the place as we can't even trust our own feelings right now. We need a "Nehemiah" whose "compass" is already headed in the right direction.

Have you allowed someone wise and spiritually strong who is willing to get in the trench with you and show you the best path for your life to see your messes? If so, who is it and how have they shown their love for you?

Can we stop and pray for a moment? Dear Heavenly Father, thank you for the sweet, awesome gift of my "Nehemiah". Thank you for his/her love for You and that he/she walks in integrity. Thank you for bringing _____ into my life. I pray that I will truly listen to his/her advice and will want to do it. Give him/her wisdom in ministering to me. Bless _____ in special way today. Amen.

Day 4 we agreed with God that because He is with us and has given us the Holy Spirit, we can be strong and we can work. Have you been obedient? Did you do some work because you felt led through the Holy Spirit? Did you find a strength you had never known before? Write how you felt after you accomplished the task.

Some of you may be so repulsed by your past behavior and lack of regard for God that to go back to that lifestyle is hardly tempting. But, for some, the pull to gravitate back to your old lifestyle is all too tempting. For most, unfortunately, there probably isn't a day that goes by that something triggers your thoughts and you find yourself back where you came from. For those who came from substance abuse, the sensation could be so strong that you even taste the substance again. For those who left a relationship, you may miss the person so deeply you can hear their words ringing in your ears. For those of you who vowed to stay away from porn, you may picture a particular scene in your head as if it was right before your eyes. For those who walked away from a form of greed and/or power, the desire to control may be too much to handle. All of these thoughts can make you feel like you are about to drown in a sea of confusing emotions. These are the moments to work. These are the moments to fight for your soul. Your enemy, Satan, isn't finished with you. He knows your weakness and is waiting for the opportune time to tempt you back to your old lifestyle. Your heart cannot be divided. You cannot allow yourself to desire both – God's way and your flesh.

Please read the timely words in Ezekiel when God prophesied that the Israelites would be home again after the Babylonian captivity. Read Ezekiel 11:17-20 and answer the following questions.

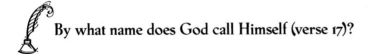 By what name does God call Himself (verse 17)?

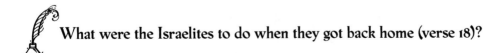 What were the Israelites to do when they got back home (verse 18)?

What kind of heart does the "Sovereign LORD" promise He will give them (verse 19)?

 What is the result of a heart of flesh (verse 20)?

When your past brings a wave of haunting feelings and emotions that tempt you to return to your old lifestyle -cry out to your Sovereign Lord. Remind yourself that He has given you an undivided heart and that you can choose to obey Him. Maybe you are the only one who knows your inner struggle and that you recently resisted temptation. Know that you have overcome and are victorious! You have gained life, integrity, Christ like character, and a glorious future! May God declare to us, "Well done, good and faithful servant" (Matthew 25:21).

Let's pray:

Dear Heavenly Father, "Teach me your way, O LORD, and I will walk in your truth; give me an undivided heart, that I may fear your name." (Psalm 86:11). In Jesus' name I pray, Amen.

PART 2
PAST

Week 3 — Who Was I?

Day 1 — In the Beginning

Today's Scripture:

In the beginning God created the heavens and the earth.

—Genesis 1:1

Not too long ago, I woke up and quickly discovered that every joint in my body was in pain. I moaned and groaned as I crawled out of bed that morning. My husband instantly knew something was wrong with me. I told him that I didn't feel sick; it just hurt to move. This pain was something I had never experienced before. I mentally went through my previous day's activities trying to recall anything I had done out of the ordinary that would have caused the pain. There seemed to be no explanation for the pain in my joints, so I made a doctor's appointment. The first doctor I visited suspected a disease that affects the heart, brain, and joints. I marveled that one particular disease could specifically attack the heart, brain, and joints. It reminded me of my spiritual condition. Sin has a unique way of causing emotional pain to one's heart, mind, and body as if it were a disease.

Child, do you feel like your heart, mind, and body hurt? Does your heart ache over your past mistakes? Does your mind hurt because at times you feel like 2 different people? Does your body hurt because of lack of care? Write how your heart, mind and body have been affected by your leaving home.

I got a second opinion about my joint pain when I went to a specialist called a rheumatologist. In order for him to clearly evaluate my joint pain, he did something highly interesting. He took a detailed inventory of my past physical health. My husband and I sat in his office answering numerous questions about my health since birth, as well as all the information I could give on my parents', grandparents', and siblings' physical health. Fascinating. The doctor did not just treat my symptoms, but took the time to find details in my childhood illnesses and with those I am blood related in order to better understand and treat my present condition.

In this week and next week's study, you will inventory your past *spiritual* and *emotional* health in order to understand your present condition. For complete wholeness and restoration of your heart, mind, and body taking inventory is extremely necessary. Some questions may be uncomfortable to answer; I need you to be truthful about yourself and circumstances. Larry Crabb in his best-selling book *Inside Out* states, "The courage to be honest is necessary if we're to experience the kind of change our Lord makes possible. Real change requires an inside look." (Larry Crabb, *Inside Out* ,Colorado Springs: Navpress,1988, p. 37.) Crabb goes on to say, "Those who refuse to honestly face their disappointment and hurts are more vulnerable to the devilish power of shallow fun to masquerade as an angel of life." (*Ibid,* p. 97.) If we want to successfully go from this season of our life as a mature, healthy man or woman of God, then addressing our past including relationships, events, traumas, beliefs, actions, and behaviors is a vital step in the journey to wholeness, peace and freedom. Just to let you know—I do not have the disease the first doctor speculated, and I am free from all joint pain! Praise the Lord!

The first five books of the Bible, known as the Pentateuch, are said to have been written by Moses during the 40 years of wandering in the desert after the Israelites left Egypt. They were not written as the events happened, but in hindsight. As Moses sat among the Israelites who were freed from bondage to slavery and on their way to the Promised Land he must have wondered, "How did all this happen?" He must have asked himself, "Where did we go wrong?" He must have questioned how God's chosen people could have been slaves to pagans, wandered in the wilderness, and were still hoping for "a land flowing with milk and honey" (Exodus 3:8).

So, where does Moses begin? At the very beginning of time. As you write out Genesis 1:1, let the words sink into your spirit afresh today.

As you sit among the rubble of your life wondering—"How did all this happen?—let's go back to the beginning of your life. I completely comprehend that I am not a licensed counselor. I am not having you accomplish on paper a formulized assignment. This Bible study is one piece of the puzzle to help you rebuild your relationship with God. I am trusting in God's promises that as you work through this Bible study God will accomplish His work in you through the Holy Spirit (Isaiah 55:11). Another promise of God I am believing for you is that the Holy Spirit will counsel you as you recall your past. Fill in the blanks to the following verses:

"I will praise the LORD, who _____ me; even at night my heart instructs me" (Psalm 16:7).

"Your statutes are my delight; they are my _____" (Psalm 19:24).

"But the _____, the Holy Spirit, whom the Father will send in my name, will teach you all things and will remind you of everything I have said to you" (John 14:26).

To begin the spiritual inventory of your past, let's concentrate today on your immediate family. Please take your time, and take this time seriously. Let's get started:

From what you know, what were your parents' circumstances when you were born? What is your birth order? Where did you live? Did you have any medical difficulties?

 Were your parents Christians?

 Does your name have significance?

 Do you have any specific memories during your first four years relating to your home life? Briefly describe any memory.

 Describe your mother.

Describe your childhood relationship with your mother. Could you trust her? Did you want to spend time with her? Did she spend time with you? Did you hide your feelings or share them openly with her?

 Describe your father.

 Describe your childhood relationship with your father. Was your father involved with your activities? Was he distant? Did he seem to understand you? Were you afraid of him?

 Were you abused, mistreated, or neglected? Or, were you loved and cared for?

Precious one, God has ordained your days. You were born exactly the moment God planned. He knows you. He knows your family and your circumstances. He is not a distant God. He is lovingly intimate with you. He is also actively involved in the details of your life. He accomplishes things on your behalf.

Let's see with new eyes God's activity in the lives of the first two persons created by reading Genesis 2:4-9, 15-25.

Record the verbs showing the specific actions God performed on behalf of Adam and Eve.

Example: Verse 7—"The LORD God *formed* the man from the dust of the ground and *breathed* into his nostrils the breath of life" (italics used to emphasize verb).

The Hebrew word for *formed* (verse 7) is compared to a potter who uses his hands to make vessels from clay. God said to Jeremiah, "Like clay in the hand of the potter, so are you in my hand, Israel" (Jeremiah 18:6). No one was created without God's involvement. Paul tells us in Acts 17:28, "For in him we live and move and have our being."

Let's pray:

For our prayer today please speak God's powerful and healing words back to Him. Dear heavenly Father, "You created my inmost being; you knit me together in my mother's womb. I praise you because I am fearfully and wonderfully made; your works are wonderful, I know that full well. My frame was not hidden from you when I was made in the secret place. When I was woven together in the depths of the earth, you saw my unformed body. All the days ordained for me were written in your book before one them came to be" (Psalm 139:13–16). In Jesus' name I pray, Amen.

Week 3 — Who Was I?

Day 2 — Your Wound

As we continue to take inventory of our spiritual and emotional history, let's keep in mind who our God is. Please look up and read the following Scriptures: Exodus 15:26; Jeremiah 17:14; and Psalm 147:3. God as the Great Physician will do what as you cry out to Him in your brokenness?

The world has numerous avenues attempting to heal your emotional wounds. You can find help from television talk shows, self-help books, magazine articles, therapists, or prescription medications. I believe God can and will use others to help us in the healing process. Just remember that in or through whomever is there to help, that source's main responsibility is to lead you to Jehovah Rapha God, our Healer. In the end, He should receive all the credit for healing you. No brother or sister in the Lord can heal like Him!

The spiritual and emotional inventory questions for today will be concerning your relationship with Jesus and the church, as well as your home life.

Today's Scripture:

Your wound is as deep as the sea. Who can heal you?

—Lamentations 2:13c

Did you attend church? Who took you to church? What was the name of your church? Do you remember any teachers?

Did you receive Jesus as your personal Lord and Savior? Were you baptized? Describe your salvation experience.

 Describe your personal relationship with Jesus in those early years as a Christian. Did you read the Bible and pray regularly? Did you hear Him speak to you? Did you obey God?

 What was your home life like? Were there any significant events?

 Did someone (neighbor, family member, adult, school friend, teacher, etc.) wound you? Did someone say something hurtful? Did someone hurt you physically, emotionally, or sexually? What happened? How did it make you feel? How does it make you feel today?

Do you know if your mom or dad was wounded in a similar way as you were? If so, what do you know about the situation?

 Did you tell anyone about your wounding? If so, how was it handled? How was it treated?

 As you look back on your wound, what do you wish you or someone you trusted could have done different to help you in your healing process?

 Can you relate to Lamentations 2:3c? Does your wound feel as if it is as "deep as the sea"? Explain.

It may feel deep because it is an area of your life you have not thought of in years. It may feel deep because you have tried to forget it. It may feel deep because you don't want anyone to know about it. It may feel deep because it has been buried underneath other wounds. It may feel deep because the pain is severe. It may feel deep because you have been carrying the pain for so many years.

Child, God wants to be your Healer TODAY! Allow Him to mend your brokenness. Right now in the quietness, pour out your hurt to Him. Tell Him everything. He wants you to release this pain and hurt to Him. "Then the woman, knowing what had happened to her, came and fell at his feet and, trembling with fear, told him the whole truth" (Mark 5:33).

Now picture yourself at the feet of Jesus receiving healing from Him. Let Him embrace you with a hug.

"He said to her, 'Daughter, your faith has healed you. Go in peace and be freed from your suffering" (Mark 5:34).

Let's pray:

Dear heavenly Father,. I believe You to be my healer. Free me today of my suffering.In Jesus' name I pray, Amen.

Week 3 — Who Was I?

Day 3 — Someone to Devour

Today's Scripture:

Be self-controlled and alert. Your enemy prowls around like a roaring lion looking for someone to devour.

—1 Peter 5:8

Statistics reveal that most of us are likely to receive salvation from Jesus Christ (become a Christian) by the age of 12. George Barna writes, "We discovered that the probability of someone embracing Jesus as his or her Savior was 32 percent for those between the ages of 5 and 12; 4 percent for those in the 13-18 range; and 6 percent for people 19 or older." (George Barna, *Transforming Children into Spiritual Champions,* Ventura:Regal Books, 2003, p.34.))

I am all for children coming to know the Lord at an early age. Jesus told the disciples, "Let the little children come to me, and do not hinder them, for the kingdom of heaven belongs to such as these" (Matthew 19:14). As parents, we pray that our children will come to know Jesus at an early age so they can grow up knowing Him, serving Him, and loving Him all their days. My husband and I were with each of our girls as they gave their life to the Lord. Those moments with them will forever be engraved on our hearts and minds; they were glorious! I love knowing my girls and I are not just blood related, but also related by Jesus' blood because He shed His so that we can belong to His family. I am deeply grateful my girls desire Jesus and understand what He has done for them on the cross. I am also completely aware that Satan does not want my girls to live out God's promised abundant life.

Before someone accepts Jesus as Lord and Savior, he or she is an enemy of God (Romans 5:10). But as soon as someone accepts Jesus, he or she has an enemy named Satan (1 Peter 5:8).

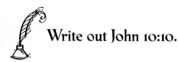 Write out John 10:10.

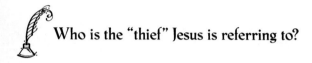 Who is the "thief" Jesus is referring to?

I wholeheartedly believe that children are not exempt from Satan's attacks and schemes. One of Satan's plans is to steal, kill, and destroy a believer's witness/testimony as an adult by attempting to steal, kill, and destroy a believer's character and beliefs during his or her childhood. To render an adult an ineffective light for the kingdom of God, Satan starts early in his or her life.

Please read the account of Mark 9:14-27 and answer the following questions.

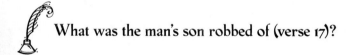 What was the man's son robbed of (verse 17)?

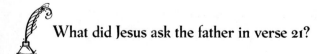 What did Jesus ask the father in verse 21?

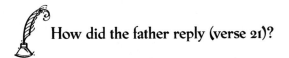 How did the father reply (verse 21)?

Jesus commanded an evil spirit to come out of the son. What did Jesus call the spirit (verse 25)?

We can assume that the man's son was at least a teenager if not older, since he answers Jesus saying his son had been in the condition since childhood. Satan had robbed the boy of his speech; then Jesus came to town and commanded the evil spirit to leave and never return. What is awesome is the boy could then use his new found voice to proclaim the good news of Jesus Christ who "lifted him to his feet" (Mark 9:27).

From this account, we learn that children are not off limits for Satan to do his work. I also can't help but mention how beautiful it was that the father brought his son to Jesus for healing. It is our responsibility as a parent to pay attention to our children in such a manner that if we notice anything unusual we can take their needs to Jesus.

Can you remember an instance in your childhood when one of your parents or caregivers noticed something unusual about you and took you to get help?

From Mark 9:14-27, what did you learn?

 From yesterday's study, did you write down a wound(s) you incurred?

 Do you see a connection to the wound and to how Satan has been attempting to kill, steal, or destroy a part of your character or beliefs? If so, how?

Most likely there is a lie from Satan associated with your wound. When we consciously or even unconsciously believe this lie, destruction soon takes place.

 Ask the Holy Spirit to reveal the lie. What do you think the lie is or what do you think it could be?

 Where did the lie originate? Did it come from yourself or someone else?

Identifying the lie is a huge step. See the lie for what it is—not truth. Lies come from our enemy, not from our heavenly Father. Our heavenly Father speaks only what is true.

Do you feel like the "someone" in 1 Peter 5:8 who Satan has found and tried to devour? Write your thoughts.

When my middle daughter, Skylar, was two-and-a-half years old she almost drowned in the pool where we were swimming. I had my back turned to Skylar, caring for her 10-month-old sister. I thought Skylar was in the baby pool. She stepped into the big pool without her life vest on and went right under the water bobbing her head up as best she could. I eventually saw her struggling and rescued her. It was a terrifying moment. I grabbed Skylar and brought her out of the water where I wrapped a towel around her and held her close. Skylar was hesitant to swim the remainder of that summer. Whenever she did swim, afterwards she would exclaim, "Mommy, I didn't even drown!"

Child, praise God, you have not been devoured! Yes, you are coming out of a season of captivity, but Satan didn't get the victory in your life! God is on your side and with Him you are victorious. The year after Skylar's swimming incident, she actually became a better swimmer because she understood water and her lack of floating ability! Her experience taught her a valuable lesson. You too are becoming a more mature believer in Christ since your homecoming!

"And the God of grace, who called you to his eternal glory in Christ, after you have suffered a little while, will himself restore you and make you strong, firm and steadfast. To him be the power for ever and ever. Amen" (1 Peter 5:10-11).

Let's pray:

Dear heavenly Father, I praise You for rescuing me from my trouble. You have the power to restore me, and make me strong, firm, and steadfast. In Jesus' name I pray, Amen.

Week 3 — Who Was I?

Day 4 — Rid of All

The purpose of examining our past is not for placing blame on others or to lead you to depression. The goal of taking a spiritual inventory of your past is clearly for your healing for your today and your tomorrows. Why bother rehashing the past? I believe it will give you genuine insight into the whys of your leaving home. It will also reveal the areas of your life Satan has been stealing, killing, and destroying, whether in subtle or obvious ways. As we discover these areas, we can deal with them appropriately and biblically, which will allow us to become whole, free, and able to love more fully. As difficult as it is to examine your past, know that you are unlocking doors Satan wanted you to keep secret. It is time to put truth in your innermost places and clean out what doesn't belong.

Jesus states a truth we need to put into practice in Matthew 23:26, "First clean the inside of the cup and dish, and then the outside also will be clean."

Today's Scripture:

Get rid of all bitterness, rage and anger, brawling and slander, along with every form of malice.

—Ephesians 4:31

 In your own words describe Jesus' words in Matthew 23:27–28.

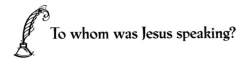 To whom was Jesus speaking?

What is more important to Jesus: the way we appear to others, or who we are on the inside (our true character)? Why do you think Jesus values one over the other?

In Matthew 15, the teachers of the law and the Pharisees had a discussion with Jesus about what makes a person "unclean.". The teachers of the law and the Pharisees argued that Jesus' disciples didn't wash their hands before they ate; therefore, that makes them unclean. According to Matthew 15:17-20, what is Jesus' answer to their argument?

I believe we can conclude that what comes out of our mouths gives evidence to what is in our hearts.

Child, what is in your heart? What have you spoken lately that has been out of anger, resentment, unforgiveness, or hatred? To whom have you spoken these words?

It may be difficult to put your harsh words on paper. We don't like to see the ugly side of ourselves. But, in our pursuit of a Christlike character, our ugliness has to go!

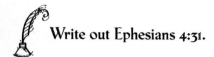 Write out Ephesians 4:31.

Ephesians 4:31 describes a progression of the heart and mind that leads to spoken words and a behavior.

From the Strong's Exhaustive Dictionary:

The word *bitterness* simply means "to pack, press down."

The word *rage* means "passion (as if breathing hard): fierceness, indignation, wrath."

The word *anger* means "desire (as a reaching forth or excitement of the mind), i.e. violent passion."

The word *brawling* means "an outcry, crying."

The word *slander* means "blasphemy, evil speaking, railing, vilification (especially against God)."

The word *malice* means "badness, i.e. depravity, or malignity, or trouble:-an evil, malice, naughtiness, wickedness."

Here's the progression: bitterness pressed down in our hearts leads to indignation (anger aroused by something unjust) that leads to rapid breathing that leads to an exalted desire in the mind that leads to crying out that leads to speaking evil of God's name, and that leads to depravity (moral corruption). Picture it like this: Bitterness is packed down in the pit of your stomach, and then when something/someone angers you, the bitterness makes its way up the esophagus. You begin to breathe harder, along with your heart pounding. Bitterness now makes it way up to your mind, and you start thinking vengeful thoughts as well as rationalizing your anger. Then the bitterness comes out of your mouth, and you lash out with regretful words. You also use your words to blame God for "not being there." Over time this lashing out becomes a bad habit causing depravity in your soul.

Does this progression look familiar to you? Have you seen this progression portrayed in yourself especially before you left home? If so, what happened?

Here's the question: What is the root cause of your bitterness? Do you remember Lamentations 2:13c from Day 2? It says, "Your wound is as deep as the sea." I am convinced that your wound is the root cause of your bitterness. How does that hit you? Do you think it could be true for you? Or do you think your root could go even deeper than your wound? Pray right now asking the Holy Spirit to lead you to truth.

Philip Yancey in *Soul Survivor* writes, "Our instinctive response to such wounding memories is to act as if they did not happen, to not talk about them and think instead about happier things. But by the deliberate act of not remembering we allow the suppressed memories to gain strength and maim or functioning as human beings."(Philip Yancey, *Soul Survivor*, New York City: Random House, Inc., p. 304.)

I want you to see an amazing Scripture from the Amplified Bible. Hebrews 12:15 reads: "Exercise foresight *and* be on the watch [look after one another], to see that no one falls back from *and* fails to secure God's grace (His unmerited favor and spiritual blessing), in order that no root of resentment (rancor, bitterness, or hatred) shoots forth and causes trouble *and* bitter torment, and the many become contaminated *and* defiled by it."

Did you notice the progression of the "root of resentment"? It resembles the progression of Ephesians 4:31 does it not? Isn't God Word beautiful? Even when God reveals the ugly in us, it brings us to a point of awe and fear of His name!

God speaks over His own, "Then will all your people be righteous and they will possess the land forever. They are the shoot I have planted, the work of my hands, for the display of my splendor" (Isaiah 60:21).

Let's pray:

Dear heavenly Father, Uproot anything in me not planted by You. I am the shoot You have planted. I desire to be a display of Your splendor. In Jesus' holy name I pray, Amen.

Week 3 — Who Was I?

Day 5 — Forgiven

Today's Scripture:

Be kind and compassionate to one another, forgiving each other, just as in Christ God forgave you.

—Ephesians 4:32

What a week, huh? You have done exceptional work! I am so proud of you! I pray as you have opened your heart toward God in prayer and study that your time has been significant, eye-opening, and life-changing. As you plowed the deep soil of your heart, I believe the Holy Spirit has done His part to reveal the areas in need of attention, Living Water, and SONlight! Although the plowing may have been uncomfortable, it will most definitely be worth it. Our heavenly Father will not leave us as we are. He will always nourish us with His Holy Word, encourage us with His presence, strengthen us with His wisdom, and bless us with His goodness.

I understand that you are in a pivotal crossroads in your life. By faith you have chosen to return to your heavenly Father believing that life with Him has to be better than your time in captivity (away from home). At the same time, the temptation to leave again may seem like an easy way out instead of dealing with your messes, relationships, and spiritual and emotional health. Please, don't give up now. Don't take the easy way out. Your future lies in what you are doing right now. Your heavenly Father has surprises waiting for you; give Him the opportunity to share them.

A familiar verse quoted by so many is significant, especially to you right now. Did you know that Jeremiah 29:11 was written specifically for the returning Israelites who had been in captivity in Babylon? Remember, these were God's people who had grieved Him through their idolatrous ways and would not listen to Jeremiah whom God sent to warn them of impending captivity. Please read with newness today the words of Jeremiah 29:10-11. Read them again, this time inserting your name in place of "you."

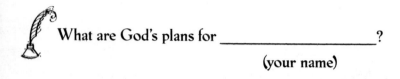

What are God's plans for _____?

(your name)

We still have some business to take care of today. I know you have been wondering when the subject of forgiveness will be brought up! Today, child, today!

Have you been surprised at all by some of your emotions, especially in regards to yesterday's study? Have you felt some anger in your heart that you didn't realize you possessed? Has your mind been filled with vengeful thoughts? Have you wanted to yell at someone (maybe even God)? What were some of your emotions that were provoked yesterday?

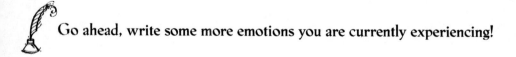

Go ahead, write some more emotions you are currently experiencing!

You have permission to be angry. You have permission to be hurt. You have permission to want revenge. You have permission to want to be violent. You have permission to feel. You have permission to cry.

"But you, O God, do see trouble and grief; you consider it to take it in hand. The victim commits himself to you; you are the helper of the fatherless" (Psalm 10:14).

 Circle the word *victim* in the above verse.

 Do you feel like a victim? Even though you know you had a part in your path to captivity, you can still *feel* like a victim because the captivity betrayed you. It backfired on you. Have you had continuous thoughts like these:

○ No one understands me.
○ No one really cares.
○ I'll never be over "this."
○ I'll never forget what he or she did.
○ I'll never be who God created me to be.
○ My life is worthless.
○ My problems are too big for anyone to help me.
○ I can't change how I feel.

 What are some other thoughts of being a victim?

 Do you want to remain feeling like a victim?

Honestly, I don't believe you desire to remain feeling like a victim. I believe you want to be a SURVIVOR. The path from victim to survivor is called forgiveness.

Yesterday we studied Ephesians 4:31. Today's Scripture is Ephesians 4:32. Please read these two Scriptures from your own Bible.

 From verse 31, list the things we are to get rid of.

 From verse 32, list the qualities we are to possess.

A victim holds on to bitterness, rage, anger, brawling, slander, and malice. A survivor has first received forgiveness from God, and then offers the same forgiveness to those who have offended them.

Let's pray:

For our prayer today, I want you to insert the name(s) of those who have hurt you, victimized you, wounded you, made fun of you, neglected you, or harmed you.

Dear heavenly Father, You have so graciously forgiven me of all my sins. Thank You for Your kindness and compassion towards me. I receive Your forgiveness. By an act of my will, in the name and under the blood of Jesus, I choose to forgive _____ for intentionally or unintentionally hurting me. I no longer hold against him or her anything he or she has done to cause me hurt or pain. I give him or her over to You, Lord, to do as You please. You are my Defender and the Avenger. I trust in You. I forgive him or her as You have forgiven me, and I bless him or her and ask Your blessing upon him or her. In Jesus' name I pray, Amen.

You, LORD, hear the desire of the afflicted; you encourage them, and you listen to their cry, defending the fatherless and the oppressed, so that mere earthly mortals will never again strike terror (Psalm 10:18).

Week 4 — What Did I Do?

Day 1 — My Way

Today's Scripture:

I warned you when you felt secure, but you said, "I will not listen!" This has been your way from your youth; you have not obeyed me.

—Jeremiah 22:21

Last week's study challenged us to go deep within ourselves and our pasts to better understand who we are today. In Day 1, we learned that God ordained for each us to occupy planet earth for this exact time, and that He is actively involved with us personally—not just from a distance. In Day 2, we discovered God can heal even the deepest of wounds. . In Day 3, we revealed that children are not exempt from the attacks of Satan, and that he knows of our wounds and uses them against us even in our adulthood. In Day 4, we uncovered some bitterness in our hearts that needed to go. In Day 5, we came to understand that because God has forgiven us, we can choose to forgive those who have hurt us.

This week's study will also challenge us deep within ourselves as we evaluate *what* we did, especially during the time before we left home.

God's people, the Israelites, took possession of the Promised Land after their slavery to the Egyptians for 400 years and after their 40 years of wandering in the desert. God performed numerous miracles to supply their needs and to keep them safe so that they could live abundantly. In the Promised Land, they were settled, safe, secure, and satisfied. God brought them into a fertile land "to eat its fruit and rich produce" (Jeremiah 2:7). Yet, in the midst of their prosperity, the Israelites began to set their eyes on the visible instead of their invisible God who had made Himself known through miracles and the prophets. God's people didn't deny God, but stopped serving and obeying Him. They also turned to Baal and other false gods in their worship. Obviously their rebellion displeased the Lord. In His anger, did He just thrust them into Babylonian captivity? Did He try to get their attention and warn them and remind them of His love for them? Did He want to send them into captivity? Did He truly understand their hearts? Jeremiah offers us insight into God's purposes.

 Look up the following verses and write what God did to get the attention of the rebellious Israelites.

 Jeremiah 5:3

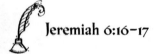 Jeremiah 6:16-17

 Jeremiah 7:13

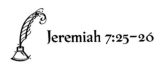 Jeremiah 7:25-26

 Jeremiah 11:7-8

 Jeremiah 26:1-5

Did you sense the seriousness in God's voice? He spoke. He warned. He sought them. He pursued them through the prophet Jeremiah. He wanted them to repent so that He could relinquish the punishment of captivity. "God had risen early and sent his servants the prophets, but Israel would not hear. Now the fate predicted for an apostate nation in Deuteronomy 28-30 was inevitable. Babylon would capture Judah. And it would be best for the people to give in gracefully and so save their lives." (Charles F. Pfeiffer, Wycliffe Bible Commentary, Chicago: Moody Press, 1990, p. 656.)

What does this have to do with us? I believe Jeremiah 22:21 gives us an amazing insight into our own rebellion. Read Jeremiah 22:21 from your Bible. Just as the Israelites refused to listen to God in their comfortable lives in the Promised Land, so we too, refused to listen to

72

His warnings. Sure, we may have obeyed Him in other areas of our life. Maybe no one even suspected your hidden rebellion because outwardly you did "all the right things." But, the area in our life that lived in rebellion toward God did not go unnoticed by God. He is not interested in partial obedience or a divided heart. God says to us, "This has been your way from your youth." This particular area of rebellion has gotten us in trouble since we were little.

Do you remember some of the warning signs God sent to get your attention? Was it a particular song on the radio? Was it an email? Was it Scripture? Was it a close friend?

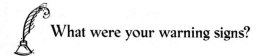 What were your warning signs?

Remember when Moses was on the mountain hearing from God and receiving the 10 commandments? What did Moses come home to (Exodus 32:1-4, 19)?

Just as the Israelites were prone to worship idols "from their youth," we, too, may have something in our childhood that opened a door to temptation even years later. . Think this one through. Last week we investigated a wound from our past. We also thought about lies that could have been said to us because of the wound. Now, I want you to think back and remember what action you took as you believed a lie. Write down some of your thoughts, and then turn it into a prayer asking God to reveal any hidden rebellion from your childhood.

Are you beginning to see some patterns in your ways? Are you beginning to see some thought patterns and behavior patterns that led up to captivity? Explain.

God wants these lies and rebellious ways (as little as they seem or as grand as they are) exposed so that we can confess it as sin, repent, and leave no more ground for temptation in these specific areas.

We've tried life our way. That life didn't turn out as fun as we had hoped. We are home now desiring to do life God's way. We can't do God's way on our own. We desperately need Him. He knows we need His divine help. God gives us a gift. "I will give them singleness of heart and action, so that they will always fear me and that all will then go well for them and for their children after them" (Jeremiah 32:39).

Let's pray:

Dear heavenly Father, I desire to leave a legacy of obedience to You and Your ways to my children and grandchildren. May my eyes look to You always. In Jesus' name I pray, Amen.

Week 4 — What Did I Do?

Day 2 — Enticed

I want to start by saying that God has much compassion for you. What you have experienced and what you are currently going through is not new to God. He has heard and seen all this before. He understands our humanness far better than even we do. Continue to come closer to your heavenly Father. Your vulnerability and humility toward God is reaching His heart! He rises in compassion to comfort you. "The LORD will surely comfort Zion and will look with compassion on all her ruins" (Isaiah 51:3). Your "ruins" or "messes" may not all be cleaned up at this point in your journey of restoration, but rest assured, God says, "My righteousness draws near speedily, my salvation is on the way" (Isaiah 51:5).

I believe I can confidently say that none of us planned on going into captivity. None of us sought destruction. None of us ever believed we would end up where we did. Who would have thought we could be an alcoholic? Who would have thought we could be pregnant before graduating from high school? Who would have thought we could become homeless? Who would have thought our bodies would be wasting away due to the lack of proper nourishment? Who would have thought we could be in the arms of someone other than our spouse? Who would have thought we could deny Jesus? Who would have thought we wouldn't walk into a church building or not see our family for months or years?

Today's Scripture:

But each person is tempted when they are dragged away by their own evil desire, and enticed.

—James 1:14

75

Let's look again at the story of the prodigal son in Luke 15. Please read verses 11-16.

This is my question. What was the lure, the bait, the enticement for the younger son? What had he heard of life outside his home? Who had he been friends with that revealed the outside pleasures? What was it for him that made him want to leave the stability of life with his father? I may not be able to answer the questions about the younger son, but I sure can answer them for myself.

What about you? When did you first get that desire to want something outside of God's will for your life? Explain your feelings.

Honestly, I believe the prodigal became a prodigal way before he ever left home. The word *prodigal* is an adjective meaning "wasteful expenditure of money, strength, or time." It can also be a noun meaning "one who is wasteful." Apparently, before the younger son asked his father for his inheritance, he had been doing a lot of wasteful thinking. He began to invest his time and strength on getting out of the house instead of using his time and thoughts to enjoy where he was.

As you think back on your desire to want something contrary to God's Word, what were some of your thoughts aiming toward the desire fulfilled? In other words, how did you plan to get what you wanted?

Here's another question I have. Why did the father give the younger son the money? The father obviously knew that it was not customary to distribute the inheritance until after he was dead. Didn't the father feel so betrayed and insulted by his own son because the son wanted his money before his death? What could have been so horrible at home that the younger son would rather have his father's money rather than his own dad? The Bible doesn't give us all these answers. Again, I know that from our personal experience we can answer the questions.

 For you, what was so bad in your relationship with Christ, that you thought leaving Him would be better for you?

For me, it was as simple as believing the lie that He wasn't enough. I had gone to church all my life, participated in Bible studies, prayed every kind of prayer you can imagine, and surrendered my life to Him, but still had unmet desires. I wanted more. I wanted more *now*!

Let's look at James 1:13-15.

 According to James 1:14 what is the beginning cause of someone being tempted?

 What two things occur after the evil desire?

In the original Greek language the words *dragged away* mean "to entice to sin."

In the original Greek language, the word *enticed* comes from the word that means "a trick, or bait." "Enticed" means "to entrap" by using bait.

We didn't plan on being tricked into a trap just as the younger son did not plan on losing all his money, becoming homeless, and nearly starving to death. But, someone else had intentions for the younger son and for us.God isn't the only one who has a plan for your life. Satan has a plan as well. I am convinced that when we begin to show signs of interest in a particular sin, our enemy, Satan, takes notice and looks for opportunities to trick us into believing that pleasures outside of God's will are good for us. We are drawn away first because of our own evil desires, then by the trickery of Satan's lies.

Michael English described being entrapped when he wrote, "This is the pattern of addiction: a gradual breakdown of boundaries so that you wind up doing things you would have never dreamed of doing and hanging around people you would have never dreamed of hanging around with. It's self-destruction by degrees, a domino effect of one stupid decision after another, each one not a huge risk in itself but, when combined, a blue-print for disaster. I hated it but was powerless to stop it, like a man lost at sea who becomes so exhausted he finally gives himself up to drown." (Michael English, *The Prodigal Comes Home,* Nashville: Thomas Nelson, 2007, p. 180.)

Conclude with the heartwarming words of Luke 15:20.

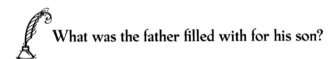 **What was the father filled with for his son?**

Your heavenly Father is filled with compassion for you. He longs to embrace you and kiss you. You are already in His lap, receive His fatherly love.

Let's pray:
For our prayer today, listen to your heavenly Father lavish His love over you as His child. Write what He is speaking to you.

> *As a father has compassion on his children, so the LORD has compassion on those who fear him; for he knows how we are formed, he remembers that we are dust* (Psalm 103:13–14).

Week 4 What Did I Do?

Day 3 — Deceived

Yesterday I had some questions concerning the younger son in the story of the prodigal son that could not be answered. I bet you have some questions, too, that have yet to be answered. Maybe one of your questions is, "Why has this happened to me?" Maybe you can say that you didn't plan on your decisions hurting so many people. Maybe you can say that you truly thought everything was going to be alright. Maybe you even thought you were in God's will even though you were actually in rebellion. That, child, is a true sign of being deceived. When we think we are in God's will, but are in the hand of the enemy, deception at its best. Yikes!

Today's Scripture:

But look, you are trusting in deceptive words that are worthless.

—Jeremiah 7:8

As the Israelites were comfortable in the Promised Land and as they began to worship idols and participate in detestable practices in direct disobedience to God, there were prophets who proclaimed that nothing would happen to them. The prophets said falsely that God wouldn't really punish them or take them from the land given to them. Unfortunately God's people listened to the prophets and continued in their detestable ways.

 According to Jeremiah 23:16 what does the Lord Almighty say the prophets fill the Israelites with?

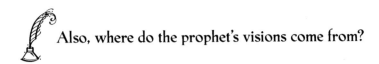 Also, where do the prophet's visions come from?

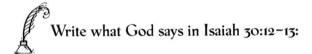 Did you hear lies, false hopes in your pursuit of fulfillment outside of God's will? Did you see others seemingly prosperous in the very area of your own rebellion? Did you hear what you wanted to hear from those doing the same destructive things you were doing? Explain.

Deception is highly dangerous. The scary thing about true deception is that what we think to be true is actually a lie. Dangerous!

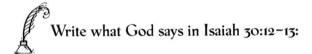 Write what God says in Isaiah 30:12-13:

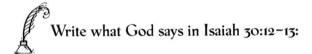 In your own words, what is the Holy One saying in the above Scripture?

God says that as we continue to reject His words and warnings, our life is going to be unrecognizable. Unrecognizable in the sense that things don't work out as we had planned. Everything around us will fall apart. Our life will look like ruins even though we were pursuing some sort of prosperity of soul.

One of my questions from yesterday's study was: "Why did the father give the younger son the money?" In my opinion, the exchange of the inheritance from the father's hand to the younger son's is the beginning of "collapse." As soon as he left his father's home, life as he once knew it became unrecognizable.

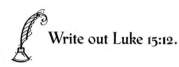 Write out Luke 15:12.

Jesus spoke in parables frequently to express truths. In this parable, we can conclude that the father represents our Father in heaven. The two sons represent those who believe in Jesus and confess Him as Lord. The two sons are saved. They are living in the house with the father; they are a part of his family. The prodigal son is not "lost" in the sense that he is not saved. He is lost in the sense that he is away from the father. The younger son could not be identified as a "prodigal" unless he was first a Christian. When we wander our thoughts, time, energy, money, off of our identity of belonging to our heavenly Father, we characterize a prodigal. "I leave home every time I lose faith in the voice that calls me the Beloved and follow the voices that offer a great variety of ways to win the love I so much desire. I am the prodigal son every time I search for unconditional love where it cannot be found." (Henri Nouwen, *The Return of the Prodigal Son,* New York: Doubleday, 1992, p.40,43).

Stay with me. I want you to see something in Scripture. It is so glorious when the Old Testament and New Testament come together creating a picture of our relationship with our Creator, our Lord.

 Look up and read Jeremiah 12:7, Jeremiah 22:25 and Jeremiah 32:28. What is the exchange that happens from God's hand?

What are the similarities of the exchange of the Israelites over to captivity in Babylon to the exchange of the younger son in a "distant country" (Luke 15:12)?

So, you answer the question: "Why did the father give the younger son the money?"

God told the Israelites in Jeremiah 17:4, "Through your own fault you will lose the inheritance I gave you. I will enslave you to your enemies in a land you do not know, for you have kindled my anger, and it will burn forever."

God has a responsibility to those who are His. He is to be worshiped! When one of His own rebels, God acts. He loves us too much to leave us in our sin. He deeply desires an intimate relationship with us. "He is a holy God; he is a jealous God" (Joshua 24:19). In God's holiness, He is jealous for us that we delight, and find pleasure in Him alone. He warns, He speaks, He pursues us, but when we refuse Him, He does what is necessary to get our attention. He will be proved right (Psalm 51:4).

Here's the good news: captivity worked. The Israelites came back home to the Promised Land and rebuilt it as it was before. The prodigal son came home!

Rejoice child! You're home! You are hearing and receiving the goodness of the Lord!

Let's pray:

Dear heavenly Father, I want to delight and find pleasure in You and Your ways alone. Thank you for being jealous for me. You love me more than I can comprehend. In Jesus' Name I pray, Amen.

Week 4 — What Did I Do?

Day 4 — Obstinate

We have learned in our previous days of study that God warns us not to continue in our destructive/sinful ways because He truly wants to bless us. Since we bear His name, He is responsible to discipline us when we continue our disobedience. On Day 1 of this week, I asked what warnings God sent you to get your attention. Somewhere along the way, we chose not to heed the warnings. For the Israelites, God sent true prophets to warn the people of captivity as well as prophecy of future restoration. Ezekiel and Jeremiah were among the prophets God used during this time.

The prophet Jeremiah was instructed by God to buy a field in Jerusalem even as the armies of Babylon were attacking Jerusalem (Jeremiah 32).

Fill in the blanks to Jeremiah 32:10 which described the transaction. "I _____ and _____ the deed, had it _____, and weighed out the silver on the scales."

This investment in Jerusalem was a sign to the people that one day "Houses, fields and vineyards will again be bought in this land" (Jeremiah 32:15). Isn't Jeremiah's purchase an amazing picture of God using someone in our life who sees beyond our destructive ways and

Today's Scripture:

But the people of Israel are not willing to listen to you because they are not willing to listen to me, for all the Israelites are hardened and obstinate.

—Ezekiel 3:7

instead to what we look like in Christ? It is a picture of someone investing in us when we are at our worst knowing that better days are ahead even if we don't believe it about ourselves.

Who is your Jeremiah? Who spoke blessings over your life in your time away from "home"?

What did you think about his or her words at the time? Did you believe him or her? Did you think he or she was clueless?

Ezekiel was a prophet sent by God to get the people's attention and to help them in their time of captivity. Ezekiel was actually among the Jews who were exiled in Babylon. Read in Ezekiel 2:1–10 of God's commissioning on Ezekiel. How did God describe the people He was sending to Ezekiel?

According to Ezekiel 3:7, why do the people not listen to Ezekiel?

When we are deceived and we think that pleasures outside of God's will can bring us fulfillment, pleasure, happiness, and hope, we push aside anything pertaining to God. In those times, we think that the world is more relevant than God and that the world's ways are wiser than God's Word. We refuse to listen to those who have anything to say about what God wants for our life. Because the life we have now chosen has deceived, intoxicated, captivated, and ensnared us into believing we are on the right path when we are actually on the path to destruction, we disregard God. Why would we want to listen to what God says when for a time sin is pleasurable? After all, it seems as if we are getting away with it? Proverbs 12:15 says, "The way of fools seems right to them."

 Paul warns his brothers in Philippians 3:18–19 of those who refuse to listen to him. In verse 18, Paul says that many live as what?

Child, don't be discouraged. Just because we may have "lived as enemies of the cross of Christ" does not mean we are still an enemy. Our hearts are now turned to Him and tuned into what His Word says to us. God is fighting for us not against us.

You may have not been able to write down someone's name who has been a Jeremiah to you, but did you know God is your Jeremiah? "He anointed us, set his seal of ownership on us, and put his Spirit in our hearts as a deposit, guaranteeing what is to come" (2 Corinthians 1:21b-22). God bought us through the blood of His Son, Jesus Christ, and deposited His Holy Spirit in our heart as an investment in our inheritance of eternal life with God our heavenly Father! God has seen you in your worst of times, seen past your destructive ways, and believed you have a beautiful future ahead of you where you will again stand strong in Christ.

Let's pray:
Write out your own prayer to God praising Him for His gift of the Holy Spirit within you.

Week 4 What Did I Do?

Day 5 — Foothold

Today's Scripture:

And do not give the devil a foothold.

—Ephesians 4:27

As we conclude Week 4's study on what we did to get us to the point of captivity, I want to encourage you by saying that you are doing a mighty work for the sake of God's Kingdom. Every day matters. What you did yesterday counts. What you do today counts toward your future. Right now, in this pivotal time in your life, you are making great strides toward a healthier, stronger, and blessed you. I so believe that the best is yet to come in your life. You have not reached the end of ministry to others; you are in the beginning. You have not been disqualified to run this race of faith in God. You have not lost your calling and purpose in ministry. Remember, none of this is new to God. He has dealt with humans for quite some time now. He knows what to do and He appreciates our cooperation!

I think you will find today's study intriguing. I don't think I could wrap up Week 4 without taking you to this small but powerful segment of Scripture in 2 Kings.

Before reading the segment, let me give you a little background information. Hezekiah was in the lineage of King David and became King of Judah in 715 B.C. and reigned for 29 years. Hezekiah trusted in the Lord and did what was right in the eyes of the Lord. One of the first things accomplished in his reign was the reopening of the temple that had been closed by his father, Ahaz. Hezekiah "held fast to the LORD and did not cease to follow him; he kept the commands the LORD had given Moses" (2 Kings 18:6). Hezekiah was considered a successful king. Towards the end of his reign Hezekiah became ill to the point of death. Through the prophet Isaiah God told Hezekiah that he would be healed as God had heard the pleas of Hezekiah.

Now please read 2 Kings 20:12-18.

Right after a mountain top experience of being healed of a terminal illness, Hezekiah makes the stupidest decision of his life that would eventually affect hundreds of thousands of God's people. See, at this time in history Babylon was not the power house, it was Assyria. Hezekiah's naivety cost the people of Judah everything.

As you think back on your time before you left home, did you have a mountain top experience with God? Did you have an unusual experience or closeness with God just prior to making a stupid decision?

I know that I can relate. I was truly on a "spiritual high" from a particular experience I had with God at a Christian camp. I too became naïve and felt that all my decisions were good. I never saw the disaster coming.

According to 2 Kings 20:12–18 what exactly was the stupid decision Hezekiah made?

Can you even believe it? Hezekiah paraded the unknown enemy all throughout his palace, and proudly, but ignorantly showed the envoys every bit of the treasures. Yikes!

The prophecy of verses 16-18 was fulfilled more than 100 years later when King Nebuchadnezzar ordered the Babylonian armies to attack Jerusalem.

One little "innocent" decision can cost us hugely. As you look back, do you recognize something significant that you did innocently that was in actuality a really stupid decision?

On Day 1 of this week, we discussed that we may have done something in our youth that opened a door for temptation later in our life. Hezekiah's decision is a perfect illustration of giving the enemy of our souls an open door—literally.

Write out Ephesians 4:27.

The word *foothold* in the NIV is the same word for "opportunity" in the NASB and the same word for "place" in the KJV. The word comes from the Greek word, *topos*, which means "a spot." It can also mean "license."

From these definitions, what is it that God wants us to know about our enemy, Satan?

This is what I learn: If we are not wise, what we do, where we go, what we say, what we listen to, what we watch, and who we are with can give Satan permission to "kill, steal, or destroy" (John 10:10) us through an open door. For the enemy to have a "license" means we are giving him the right to rob us of treasures that were meant to be used to glorify God and to serve one another. Satan will seize the opportunity and attack at just the right moment of our weakness. Satan is patient; he waits for the time when we least expect and when the most harm can be done. Psalm 71:10 says, "For my enemies speak against me; those who *wait* to kill me conspire together" (italics mine).

 Child, let's not give the enemy a license to use his schemes against us any longer. Skim over 2 Corinthians 2:5–11. What is the main subject matter?

 What does Paul say Satan can do when we are unforgiving (verse 11)?

Forgiving others who have hurt us shuts a door to the enemy!

Let's pray:

For our prayer today, let's shut some doors. Dear heavenly Father, I don't want to give Satan permission in my life to steal, kill, or destroy anything from me. I pray that You would bring to my mind anyone I need to forgive. I choose today to forgive _____

_____ *(Insert person(s) name(s) God brings to your mind) understanding that he or she knows not what he or she has done. I choose also to forgive myself for any and all stupid decisions I have made. Make me aware of the schemes of the devil in my life. Thank You for forgiving me. I love you. In Jesus' name I pray, Amen.*

PART 3
FUTURE

Week 5 | Who Will I Be?

Day 1 — Redeemed

For the next two weeks our study will concentrate on your future. We began this Bible study focusing on your present—moving forward one-step-at-a-time. I want you to understand that the little things you do now that come from a healthy mentality are giant steps toward a healthier future.

When I was first back home from captivity, the little things like watering the flowers and doing the dishes were monumental for me because it was proof that I was home. Not only that, I also enjoyed doing the little things again because I had a new appreciation for home.

When you first came back home, what were the little things you enjoyed again?

Today's Scripture:

Let the redeemed of the
Lord tell their story—
those he redeemed from
the hand of the foe.

—Psalm 107:2

Our study in Weeks 3 and 4 focused on your past. I believe that identifying the source of our leaving home will most likely prevent us from leaving home again. I surely do not want to make the same mistakes again, and I know you do not either. I have learned that the more I understand myself—knowing my strengths, weaknesses—I can be more successful in the goals for my life. As I examined the whys and hows of the capabilities of my actions that stemmed from an unhealthy mentality and emotions, I became more aware of the necessity of daily renewal of my mind and heart.

 Have you discovered areas in your mind and emotions that could be identified as unhealthy?

As we continue to recognize unhealthy thoughts and feelings within ourselves, I pray that we are also learning to resist acting/reacting primarily out of our false-driven emotions, but rather from what we know to be right or true. I know all too well that sometimes what feels right with my heart doesn't feel right with my head. During those moments, I pause and examine my heart knowing I can't trust it right now. I then decide to go with what my head is telling me.

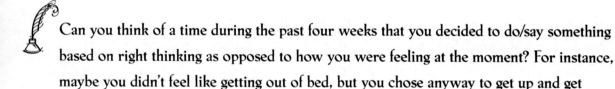 Can you think of a time during the past four weeks that you decided to do/say something based on right thinking as opposed to how you were feeling at the moment? For instance, maybe you didn't feel like getting out of bed, but you chose anyway to get up and get your day started?

Restoration of your mind, body, soul, and spirit has begun, dear child. Your wounds are healing. Never give up! During your times of rest, think about your future; picture yourself healthy making right decisions. During your times of work, know that it is not in vain. As you do the little things, you are building strong spiritual muscles. Your spiritual muscles shrunk when you were away from home. Every spiritual exercise you do strengthens your mind, body, soul, and spirit arming you to fight the fight and keep the faith. Sure, you will have scars. Even Jesus has scars. Our scars and Jesus' scars are proof of what God has done for us.

Psalm 126 is part of the "songs of ascent." These were songs that the Israelites sang as they made their annual journey to Jerusalem for Passover. The songs of ascents are also said to have been sung as the Israelites made their journey back home to Jerusalem after the 70 years of Babylonian captivity. Please read from your Bible and soak up the lyrics of Psalm 126.

"The LORD has done great things" for you.

 Write what He has done for you as you recall your journey home.

Let's not keep what God has done for us to ourselves. Let's proclaim it from the rooftops! Let's sing about them with our loudest voice! We don't need to go into detail as to all the mistakes we made. The point is not what we have done, but what God has done for us.

I love what King Nebuchadnezzar confesses to his people just after God rescued Shadrach, Meshach, and Abednego from the fiery furnace: "It is my pleasure to tell you about the miraculous signs and wonders that the Most High God has performed for me" (Daniel 4:2). Isn't that awesome?

We may never be able to say we have a squeaky-clean track record, but we can say: "But God has done great things for me."

Since your homecoming, I believe something else will change (if it hasn't already) in regard to the way you refer to your life—and that is your timeline. Just as someone refers to a life-altering car wreck, one says "before my accident," "at the time of my accident," and "after my accident." As you view your life-changing experience, you will divide the time between before, during, and after your captivity. Jot down the dates of your timeline of the years before you left home, the time away, and when you returned.

According to Jeremiah 16:14what was the main cause for celebration for the people of God?

 According to Jeremiah 16:15 what became the new main cause for celebration?

You ready for this? You want to see something awesome in Scripture? Please read the genealogy of Jesus as recorded in Matthew 1:1-17.

 What is the one and only event listed in the genealogy?

Child, our identities will be forever marked by what God had done for us when He rescued, us from our own destructive ways to living gloriously back in the house with Him, our heavenly Father. Do you know what I think our heavenly Father wants to do as He acknowledges where we have been, where we are now, and where we are going? I think He wants to throw a party! "But the father said to his servants, 'Quick! Bring the best robe and put it on him. Put a ring on his finger and sandals on his feet. Bring the fattened calf and kill it. Let's have a feast and celebrate. For this son of mine was dead and is alive again; he was lost and is found.' So they began to celebrate" (Luke 15:22-24).

Let's pray:
For our prayer today, as one who is redeemed from your sins, join the celebration with your Father and proclaim His great things He has done for you with a loud voice.

Week 5 — Who Will I Be?

Day 2 — For His Name's Sake

Today's Scripture:

He restores my soul; He guides me in the paths of righteousness for his name's sake.

—Psalm 23:3

Deep down each of us has a desire to be known. We want to be "somebody." We crave validation of who we are. We may not necessarily want to be famous, but we want to be appreciated for who we are and what we can do. In today's society, with so much focus, praise and accolades given to the talented singers, dancers, actors, it stirs in us a desire to be noticed. To have someone recognize us for our beauty, talent, or brilliant mind would make us feel special and even worthy to be alive. Maybe when you left home, you were in search of making a name for yourself. Maybe you wanted to finally be recognized for particular qualities you possess. Or maybe you were in search of wanting just to be liked. Maybe you felt unnoticed and needed more attention. Maybe the thought of being a part of a specific group of people would finally give you the feeling of being chosen, of feeling important. As we read about the younger son in the parable of the prodigal in Luke 15, we can assume that even he was on a quest to "find himself" in the distant country. The unknown of the distant country held high hopes of unbroken promises and dreams fulfilled, yet only to find each of those shattered sooner than anyone could have known. "When Luke writes 'and left for a distant country,' he indicates much more than the desire of a young man to see more of the world. He speaks about a drastic cutting loose from the way of living, thinking, and acting that has been handed down to him from generation to generation as a sacred legacy. The 'distant country' is the world in which everything considered holy at home is disregarded." (Henri Nowen, *The Return of the Prodigal Son*, New York: Doubleday, 1992, p. 33.) In the midst of the younger son's shattered life, he came to his senses and with new eyes made a quest back home.

 How do you relate to the younger son as you sought a distant country in search to find yourself?

Now that you are home, how are the distant country attractions not so attractive anymore?

It is serious business being a Christian. At whatever age we said "yes" to God's invitation to belong to His family by accepting Jesus into our heart and believing that Jesus died for our sins and was raised to life knowing we will spend eternity in heaven with God is a commitment God honors. Just a few of the numerous acts He accomplishes for us are: writes our name in the Lamb's Book of Life, seals us with the promise of the Holy Spirit, and adopts as His child. Salvation is a free gift; not one we earn. He knocks on the door of our heart and by a choice of our will we decide to let Him in. After that, He isn't going anywhere. He loves us with a passion we can't comprehend or estimate. That's why He won't leave you alone. Have you ever cried out to God by saying, "Just leave me alone"? I have. I wanted to do what I wanted to do and with no consequences. God can't leave us alone; it is impossible for Him. It is who He is; forever with us. He is Emmanuel—God with us.

 Fill in the blanks to 1 Samuel 12:22:

For the _____ of _____ _____ _____ the LORD will not reject his people,

because the LORD was _____ to make _____ _____ _____.

Belonging to the family of God means we bear His name. We represent Him. Just as a baby is given the last name of his or her father when he or she is born, we too spiritually inherit God's name. In the gospel of John, John speaks of our adoption, "Yet to all who did receive him, to those who believed in his name, he gave the right to become children of God—children born not of natural descent, nor of human decision or a husband's will, but born of God" (John 1:12-13).

Because we are God's child and represent Him, His name is 'on the line'. If we proclaim we are a Christian but act contrary, then He is responsible to punish us in such a way that has a purpose of getting us to come to our senses. He has a reputation to keep. He will not be mocked!

 According to Psalm 106:8 what two reasons does God save us?

Let's see this same theme of Psalm 106:8 carried out in Ezekiel. Remember, Ezekiel was one of the true prophets of God sent to the Israelites in their time of captivity in Babylon. Read the words God spoke to Ezekiel in Ezekiel 36:16-23.

 What did the Lord have concern for (verse 21)?

Whose name was He *not* concerned about (verse 22)?

Whose name was He concerned about (verse 22)?

What will the nations know after He does His works (verse 23)?

Have you figured out too that He alone is LORD? We have those moments tucked away in our heart of when we realized He is God and we are not. Describe a moment when you knew beyond a shadow of doubt that your God was God and you were not.

Please read with me one more passage of Scripture: Luke 15:17-21.

The younger son thought of a speech he could say to his father (verses 18–19) when he saw him again. Did the father hear the entire speech planned by the younger son (verse 21–22)?

Just like we can't earn our salvation, we can't earn our homecoming party! This is the beauty of God's grace; He favors us when we don't deserve it. The father didn't pay any attention to the whiny voice of the younger son. For you see, it was for the sake of the father's name that the son was able to come back home. "It might sound strange, but God wants to find me as much as, if not more than, I want to find God. Yes, God needs me as much as I need God. God is not a patriarch who stays home, doesn't move, and expects his children to come to him, apologize for their aberrant behavior, beg for forgiveness, and promise to do better. To the contrary, he leaves the house, ignoring his dignity by running toward them, pays no heed to apologies and promises of change, and brings them to the table richly prepared for them." (Henri Nowen, *Return of the Prodigal Son*, New York: Doubleday, p. 100.)

We may have left home in search of a name for ourselves only to find our true name is found living in Christ. Embrace God's extravagant grace.

Let's pray:

Dear heavenly Father, thank You for running to get me and accepting me as I am. I understand that You have redeemed me for Your name's sake. May I honor You with my life. In Jesus' name I pray, Amen.

I, even I, am he who blots out your transgressions for my own sake, and remembers your sins no more (Isaiah 43:25).

Week 5 — Who Will I Be?

Day 3 — Inherit a Blessing

I can't avoid it anymore. Today's study is probably not going to be one of my favorites, but one that is important. This one may be more difficult to get through because of personal hurts. As God has tenderly comforted me in this area, I pray He will use me to help comfort you (2 Corinthians 1:4).

Let's get started. Please read the rest of the story of the parable of the younger son in Luke 15:25-31.

 List what you learn about "big brother." Include character traits of who he is and who he is not.

Today's Scripture:

Do not repay evil with evil or insult with insult. On the contrary, repay evil with blessing, because to this you were called so that you may inherit a blessing.

—1 Peter 3:9

Big brother is busy, huh? Simply amazing how busyness can creep into someone's life and rob him or her of a good party. Big brother is angry. Too angry, in fact, to attend the celebration. Big brother is jealous. He is so busy thinking about what he has missed out on in the past that he can't enjoy the party in the present. Big brother is obedient to his father, but only views it as "slavery" (15:29). I guess he is in too much bondage to dance. Big brother is having his own party—a pity party.

The challenge for both sons is living under the same roof.

"Big brother won't mind if you come back as long as you hang your head and wear your shame. But when God has the audacity to give you a little dignity back and you dare lift your radiant face to heaven in liberated praise, big brother may be appalled!" (Beth Moore, *When Godly People Do Ungodly Things* Nashville: Broadman and Holman Publishers, 2002, p.288.)

We are more than likely going to be related to, go to church with, attend school with, live near, or work with someone who is like "big brother." From Scripture, let's gather some more information about these types of people of whom God has called us to be family with.

 According to the following verses, how do those described in these verses resemble big brother?

Luke 11:42

Luke 18:9-14

Matthew 23:13

Matthew 23:28

 What similar characteristic of a Pharisee is described in each of these verses?

Luke 11:38, 53-54; 14:1

Just as it didn't seem fair to big brother that he must live with the younger son, so it doesn't seem fair that we must deal with big brother. Unfortunately, we bring out the worst in him, and he brings out the worst in us.

Whoever "big brother" is in your life right now, I am sure you have noticed he is watching you. Don't let the pride in his eyes keep you from radiating Christ's love. Don't let his intimidating spirit keep you from shining forth His righteousness. Child, you are not on trial. You have nothing to prove. Remember you did nothing to earn your homecoming party, but to show up and receive the many blessings God so graciously lavished on you. Keep your head up. You are covered in Christ's blood shed for you on the cross. Your life is hidden in Christ.

We have a blessing reserved just for us. Please read 1 Peter 3:8–12. What are the ways we are to live with big brother?

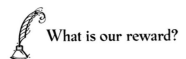 What is our reward?

Yes, big brother's eyes are on you and his ears are listening for something to accuse you of, BUT God's "eyes . . . are on the righteous and his ears are attentive to their prayer" (1 Peter 3:12).

Let's pray:

For our prayer today, allow me to pray over you. "May the LORD repay you for what you have done. May you be richly rewarded by the LORD, the God of Israel, under whose wings you have come to take refuge" (Ruth 2:12).

Week 5 — Who Will I Be?

Day 4 — Wise

Have you ever heard the saying, "My momma didn't raise no fool"? When it comes down to the end of our lives, no one wants to be in the fool category. Another saying is: "Hindsight is always 20/20." I imagine that saying could even be true for a fool. Making decisions, having discernment, and knowing what to do can be extremely confusing at times. For us who have made a wrong turn in life when we were sure it was the right turn, decisions concerning our future can be more difficult because we realized our heart cannot always be trusted.

Each one of us is desperate for wisdom. When all is said and done, we want to be known as a wise person.

As we think about who we want to be in the future, we need to understand it is important to be that person today. Who we are today applies toward our future. I have said it before and I will say it again: EVERY DAY MATTERS!

Please read the short chapter of Proverbs 9.

Today's Scripture:

Listen to my instruction and be wise; do not disregard it.

—Proverbs 8:33

 What two characters are described (verses 1 and 13)?

 Where could each character lead you (verses 6 and 18)?

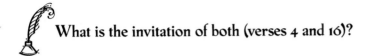 What is the invitation of both (verses 4 and 16)?

What do you personally learn about their invitations?

Who is Wisdom looking for (verse 4)?

Who is the Woman of Folly looking for (verses 15 and 16)?

Both Wisdom and Folly are located at "the highest point of the city" (3 and 14) looking for persons who are simple and lack judgment. The word *simple* in the Hebrew means "silly" and "seducible." To "lack judgment" means that one needs understanding. At particular seasons and ages of our lives, we may be more naïve and more easily seduced because we lack maturity and knowledge. Somehow it is even noticed by others.

I thought it was interesting that in verse 15 Folly is looking for those who "go straight on their way." The word *straight* in the Hebrew means: "to be straight or even; to be right, pleasant, prosperous: direct, fit, seem good, please, be right, bring straight, be upright." I can't help but think of us as we headed straight into our captivity thinking that the road seemed right. We walked right past Wisdom and into the arms of Folly. Folly seduced us with her words and sank her venom deep into our souls.

We have miraculously been given another chance from our heavenly Father. This go 'round let's walk right past Folly and go head first toward Wisdom.

Unfortunately, Folly will still be there. Choices, opportunities, and temptations will not miraculously disappear. When Folly is calling your name, take the even higher road and hear the voice of Wisdom.

 What do we *not* want to be like according to 2 Peter 2:22?

 Record from each verse what a wise person does?

Proverbs 12:1, 15

Proverbs 13:1, 20

In closing I want to share with you poem by Portia Nelson that any one of us could have written about our own experiences. It is called "An Autobiography in Five Short Chapters."

Chapter 1

I walked down the street.

There is a deep hole in the sidewalk.

I fall in.

I am lost . . . I am helpless.

It isn't my fault.

It takes forever to find a way out.

Chapter 2

I walk down the same street.

There is a deep hole in the sidewalk.

I pretend I don't see it.

I fall in, again.

I can't believe I am in the same place.

But it isn't my fault.

It still takes a long time to get out.

Chapter 3

I walk down the same street.

There is a deep hole in the sidewalk.

I see it is there.

I fall in . . . it's a habit . . . but, my eyes are
   open.

I know where I am.

It is my fault.

I get out but it still takes a long time.

Chapter 4

I walk down the same street.

There is a deep hole in the sidewalk.

 I walk around it.

Chapter 5

I walk down a different street.

(Portia Nelson, *There's a Hole in My Sidewalk*, Hillsboro: Beyond Words Publishing, 1933, p.2-3.)

Let's pray:

Dear heavenly Father, Thank You for rescuing me from my own "deep hole". I cry to You for wisdom and understanding. Lead me to quiet rest for my soul. In You I trust. In Jesus' name I pray, Amen.

Week 5 — Who Will I Be?

Day 5 — Vindicated

I pray you have already soaked up the truths taught and truly see that not only do you have a future, but that you have a bright future! You are a survivor. You have braved the toughest battles. Your life has not ended, nor your faith. You are a victorious warrior. The enemy of your soul didn't win. You are on the Lord's side, and the Lord is on your side. You are following the Commander in Chief of your life, and He leads you "beside quiet waters" (Psalm 23:2). Your future is one of rest. Rest for your weary soul. Rest from your enemies. Rest for your heart.

 How does that sound to you? Are you ready for some rest? What would you look like to be at rest? Describe yourself mentally and emotionally at rest.

Today's Scripture:

No weapon forged against you will prevail, and you will refute every tongue that accuses you. This is the heritage of the servants of the LORD, and this is their vindication from me' declares the LORD.

—Isaiah 54:17

When Nebuchadnezzar's army attacked Judah, not all were taken captive to Babylon. In fact, it didn't even happen all at one time. There were several sieges of the land. In the end, Jerusalem and the nearby towns were razed to the ground. The population was desolate. Some inhabitants escaped and found existence in fortified cities such as

Egypt. Some died of starvation and disease. Some were executed. Some died in battle. Here's the amazing truth—the ones taken from their homeland into exile were hand-picked. "The Jews living in Babylon represented the cream of their country's political, ecclesiastical, and intellectual leadership-which is why they were selected for deportation." (John Bright, *History of Israel,* Louisville:Westminster John Knox Press, 2000, p.345) They were what you might call "trophies" of Israel. The number of those deported was not a large number. It is estimated in Jeremiah 52:28-30 that 4,600 males were taken (the number does not include the women and children). "But these exiles, though few in number, were the ones who would shape Israel's future, both giving to her faith its new direction and providing impulse for the ultimate restoration of the Jewish community in Palestine." (*Ibid.*)

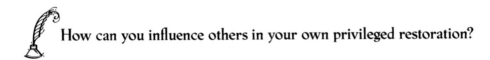 How can you influence others in your own privileged restoration?

Not all the Jews exiled returned home; some stayed in Babylon. Those chosen to return were also handpicked. This time not handpicked by the enemy, but by the hand of God. See for yourself.

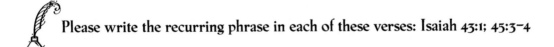 Please write the recurring phrase in each of these verses: Isaiah 43:1; 45:3-4

The God of the universe, the Maker of the heavens and the earth summoned us, called us by name! He came to our rescue and led us home. "For I am the LORD your God who takes hold of your right hand, and says to you, Do not fear; I will help you." (Isaiah 41:13).

Child, you are among the chosen to be home. All that you have been through has a divine purpose. "Exile was seen, therefore, not just as a penalty to be paid by Israel or a condition from which she was to be delivered. Rather, Israel's faithful endurance of exile and her victorious emergence from it were designed to make her a light to the nations." (Ralph W. Klein, *Israel in Exile*, Philadelphia: Fortress Press, 1979, *p.124.*).

 We read in three verses of Isaiah that God "summons us by name." What does it mean to you when you read that God, Himself, calls you by name?

You can almost hear the Lord say your full name just as a parent says your full name in a reproving tone when you get caught doing something wrong. God knows we are guilty. We know we are guilty just as the psalmist David acknowledged to God after his sin of adultery: "Against you, you only, have I sinned and done what is evil in your sight; so that you are right in your verdict and justified when you judge" (Psalm 51:4).

God found us in our captivity, summoned us by name, then led us home. The enemy tried to get the best of you…he wanted the best of you. Your best though is exemplified as you rise above your sin. Then, instead of you wearing shame, the enemy is covered in it.

Micah 7:8-10 gives us insight.

 To whom is Micah speaking? (verse 8)?

 Who did he sin against? (verse 9)

What three things does the Lord do for Micah (verse 9)?

 What will Micah see (verse 9)?

 What will his enemy see (verse 10)?

 What will his enemy be covered with (verse 10)?

 Please read also the words of Isaiah in Isaiah 50:7–9 as he portrays the same insightfulness.

What two characteristics does Isaiah say will not be on him? (verse 7)

 How does he describe God? (verse 8)

 According to Isaiah 54:17, what is our heritage and our vindication from the Lord?

If or when someone tries to point his or her finger at you and accuse you of what God has already forgiven and freed you from, God promises we will know what to say. What we say is what God has done for us. Because of God's righteousness we are redeemed from any guilt, shame, or disgrace. As we reveal God's glory in our lives, we will shine for Him. We will be light to the nations. We will be a people at rest.

Let's pray:

Dear heavenly Father, thank You for summoning me and leading me by Your hand. Thank You for choosing me to be Yours forever. Thank You for vindicating me, clearing me of accusation from the enemy by Your righteousness. In Jesus' name I pray, Amen.

Week 6 — What Will I Do?

Day 1 — Worked with All Their Heart

I can't express how much I have enjoyed studying God's Word with you. The concepts of each day's studies are forever marked in my being. God's tender words have penetrated deeply piercing even the places of my soul that had yet to be exposed. I am a changed woman. There is less of me and more of God.

Today's Scripture:

So we rebuilt the wall till all of it reached half its height, for the people worked with all their heart.

—Nehemiah 4:6

 What about you? How are you changed from the concepts studied in God's Word? What is "less" of you? What is more of God in you?

We've concentrated our Old Testament studies on the Scriptures pertaining to the Babylonian captivity. God's people were taken into *physical* captivity exiled to another country. They were released when King Cyrus of Persia declared the captives free to go back home to Jerusalem. The returning exiles did *external* work as they rebuilt their homeland. From the work of their hands, the Israelites rebuilt the temple, their homes, as well as the wall surrounding the city.

Our studies also concentrated in the New Testament in Luke 15 on the exit and return of the prodigal son. The younger son was in *spiritual* captivity. He left home based on the condition of his heart and mind, not because someone physically drove him away. When the younger son returned home, he had *internal* work to do. He didn't need to rebuild his church, home, or a surrounding wall, instead he needed to focus on the rebuilding of his inner man. It was his belief system that needed an overhaul. As the Israelites came home to literal ruins and rubble from demolished structures, the younger son came home with a shattered soul.

So, in the Old Testament, we saw physical captivity, which led to external work. In the New Testament, we see spiritual captivity, which leads to internal work.

We can certainly relate to both the Israelites in the Old Testament and the prodigal son in the New Testament. We may not have been physically driven from our intimate relationship with our Lord, but we have most assuredly were enticed away. The rebuilding and restoring of our "temple" and "wall" has been the internal work of strengthening our hearts and minds through the power of the Holy Spirit. Maybe even our physical bodies needed nourishment and care.

Spiritual captivity is no little thing. It is real, and it is life-threatening. You and I are on the battlefield each and every day. Life is a battle; not a game. We are absolutely on the winning side, but that does not mean we don't fight. We can choose offense or defense. Choosing the latter means we make our move based on what our enemy strategizes first. Child, let's stop playing "defense" and move to the offensive side. Let's move forward toward our goal of heaven with the enemy on the defensive. How about it? You in? Great! Let's huddle up and see what our Commander instructs today.

In ancient times, every city had an immensely large wall surrounding it. The wall's main purpose was to protect the people inside from being attacked by intruders. Let's examine for a moment what an ancient wall could symbolize for us spiritually.

 According to the following Scriptures, what do you conclude the "wall" to symbolize?

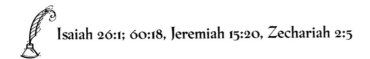 Isaiah 26:1; 60:18, Jeremiah 15:20, Zechariah 2:5

Our "wall" is a means of protection from our spiritual enemy, Satan, who desires to invade our souls with his darkness. We can't protect ourselves apart from Christ. We can't make our wall a wall of pride thinking our best efforts will be enough protection. Pride says:

- ◯ I can do it on my own.
- ◯ I don't need anyone else.
- ◯ I am strong enough.
- ◯ I won't fall again.
- ◯ I won't trust anyone again.
- ◯ I won't love anyone else again.
- ◯ I refuse to let anyone else know me.

 Can you think of something else "Pride" says?

From the above Scriptures, I believe we learn that it is simply who we are in Christ that is our wall of protection. As we hide ourselves in Christ, He is the wall between our enemy and us. Trusting God for our salvation——protects us from lies the enemy throws our way. Beleiving God's truth about who we are in Christ gives us strength to overcome the evil one.

Remember in Week 2, Day 3 we read about Nehemiah who left his job as the cupbearer to the king to help the returning Israelites rebuild the wall around Jerusalem? Let's look at the continuation of the rebuilding of the wall. Please read Nehemiah 4:1-3.

In your own words what is happening in this scene?

 Have you had similar ridicule spoken over you? If so, what was said?

Satan isn't finished with you. He, too, has a plan for your life. And....it ain't good! Satan will bring whatever opposition possible your way to prevent you from rebuilding your relationship with your heavenly Father. Satan really doesn't care *how* you give up on Christ, just as long as you do.

Let's continue our reading in Nehemiah. Please read Nehemiah 4:4-18.

 What is your favorite part of this story or favorite verse? Why?

My favorite is verse 17. What an amazing task the workers accomplished with one hand on the materials and one hand holding a weapon! I love that! When I first returned home, I was glad to be back home, but also knew that my enemy wasn't finished with me. I knew my weaknesses were still weaknesses for me. This go 'round I wanted to do it right. So I fought every second of the day to choose God's way over my own.

As you build up your inner man and become more intimate in your relationship with Christ, you are fortifying yourself to resist Satan and internal temptations. And you know what? God never gives up on you. He believes in you and thinks highly of even the littlest step you take in the right direction. What someone else may deem "insignificant," God sees as a huge victory. With all your heart, keep picking up the pieces of your rubble one piece at a time to rebuild your love relationship with Christ and to protect your soul from the enemy.

"But you are a shield around me, O LORD; you bestow glory on me and lift up my head" (Psalm 3:3).

Let's pray:

Dear heavenly Father, thank You for fighting for me. Thank You for giving me the weapons I need to fight my enemy. You are my Hero, my Rescuer, my Deliverer, my Fortress, and the One I trust. In Jesus' name I pray, Amen.

Week 6 | What Will I Do?

Day 2 — Struggle

Yesterday's study focused on the Israelites as they worked eagerly and effectively to rebuild the enormous wall around Jerusalem. Their extensive work was mostly physical labor to protect them and their families from invading enemies. We also saw that they had mental opposition from neighboring officials ridiculing them for their work. Yet, they kept building with materials in one hand and a weapon in the other, and finished the wall in a record 52 days!

We noted, too, that the necessary work for the younger son in the story of the prodigal son was internal as he experienced spiritual captivity. For our study today, we will explore more of what the New Testament teaches us concerning our rebuilding and fortifying of our heart, soul, mind, and spirit (our inner person).

Keep in mind the truth that we are in a war for our own soul knowing Satan is against us and desires to render us ineffective for God's kingdom. Now more than ever we need stay alert to Satan's schemes and learn how to combat. What is of high importance is understanding that when someone wrongs us or tempts us toward evil, our fight doesn't become about that particular person. When our anger arises or our lusts surface, we need not direct our energies negatively at another human being, but realize who our real enemy is in that

Today's Scripture:

For our struggle is not against flesh and blood, but against the rulers, against the authorities, against the powers of this dark world and against the spiritual forces of evil in the heavenly realms.

—Ephesians 6:12

particular situation. Our natural response is to lash back or to give in to temptation. But there truly is a way out that leads to victory.

Let's see what Paul has to teach us in 2 Corinthians 10:3–4. What are our weapons *not* and what *are* they?

In your opinion, what are weapons the "world" uses to fight against someone or something?

How is "divine power" different?

One of the numerous inheritances we have from our heavenly Father is His power in us. Even when our natural or human tendencies strongly flare up, we can know that His power in us is always more powerful and capable of overcoming our enemy. Surrendering our impulses over to God's mighty power is a worthwhile trade-off.

What does Ephesians 6:10 tell us to be strong in?

We will struggle, but we can be strong in our weakest moments. We don't have to give in to our anger or lust or need for revenge. It isn't that we will have "superhuman" powers. Instead, we get supernatural power from God as we seek Him in our time of struggle. God's divine power enables us to have a new and victorious battle plan as we fight on the battlefield of life.

Please read Ephesians 6:11-12.

 According to verse 11, what are we to stand against?

The first part of our battle plan is being aware of Satan's schemes—his deception. Child, whatever lies worked in the past on you, Satan will try to use again on you. The more you resist his sneaky lies, the less those lies became temptations for you.

 As you think back on your departure of home, can you identify the scheme of Satan? In other words, can you now see what was not-so-obvious at the time the subtleties of Satan's tricks that led up to your being fully deceived? Since you have been home, has some of the old lies snuck up on you again?

 According to Ephesians 6:12, what is our struggle not against and what is it against?

The second part of our battle plan is knowing who we are fighting. We can clearly see that even though we may have a problem against another human being, we don't use "worldly" weapons to win. A good question to ask yourself when being confronted with a difficult person or problem is: What is Satan's plan for me? We are usually quick to wonder about God's will for our lives without realizing Satan has a will for our life as well. When we evaluate that Satan could be using a person's words or actions to harm us, our anger or lusts diminish toward the particular person and instead we can see the bigger picture. There really is more going on in the heavenly realms! There is a war for your soul. Our struggle is against the "spiritual forces of evil." The list you identified earlier of who our struggle is against is actually a list of Satan's demons as they are ranked. The Bible Knowledge Commentary describes the list as "the spiritual 'Mafia'" (John F. Walvoord, and Roy B. Zuck, *The Bible Knowledge Commentary*, Colorado Springs: Victor, 1983, p. 643.).

Want to see this whole thing in action? Please read Matthew 16:21-23.

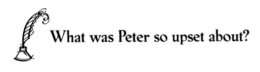
What was Peter so upset about?

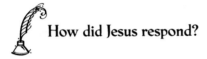
How did Jesus respond?

The Amplified Bible puts it this way, "Get behind Me, Satan! You are in My way [an offense and a hindrance and a snare to Me]; for you are minding what partakes not of the nature *and* quality of God, but of men."

Ephesians 6:13 also gives us more insight into our battle plan against evil forces. What are we to "put on"?

Continue reading verses 14-18.

 In verses 10–18, how many times does the text mention the word *stand*?

"Stand" is an important word to me; I hope it is to you as well. I am standing. I may have fallen momentarily, but now I am standing! In Christ alone and through His mercies and His grace, I am able to stand. Stand tall, dear child, the war is not over. Use your spiritual weapons and see the Lord's mighty power work through you!

Let's pray:
Dear heavenly Father, my enemy may have knocked me down, but in You I have risen. Show me Your power through me. In Jesus' name, I pray, Amen.

Week 6 | What Will I Do?

Day 3 — Again

Have you doubted your worth of service to God? Have you felt unusable? Does it seem like you have gone too far that God's calling on your life has now been revoked? Have you assumed that God's "Plan A" for your life has been scratched and He now has to default to "Plan B"? Well, put those doubts and feelings far from you! Today's study will prove to us that God is not like man. God's ways are far and above anything we can imagine. We tend to think in human terms (because, of course, we are human) putting human limitations and restrictions on ourselves and others, but God . . . .

According to Micah 7:18–19, "but God" what? What God-like things does He do for you and me?

Today's Scripture:

This is what the LORD *Almighty says: "In this place, desolate and without people or animals—in all its towns there will again be pastures for shepherds to rest flocks."*

—Jeremiah 33:12

Child, God is not still angry with you. He has pity for you and finds delight in favoring you with His mercy and compassion. He really does unconditionally love you. In fact, I will go as far to say that He has missed you. He truly is unlike any human being.

I remember a pivotal time in my life just after my decision to return home. I was having a pity party where doubt was apparently the only one invited. I doubted I would ever serve the Lord with the gifts and callings He had given me before I "left home." I felt like God had passed me by and that I would now have to rediscover gifts and a calling. I was becoming depressed and found myself taking naps during the day feeling like I had nothing to offer anyone. Then, out of nowhere, I got a call from an individual wanting me to come serve at her church for a weekend retreat. I felt the favor of the Lord on me at that moment and responded to the invitation with an affirmative. The phone call changed the theme of my party from "pity" to "praise." I broke out into complete compulsory praise to the One who showed me compassion and brought hope back into my life.

Fill in the blanks to Jeremiah 31:3–5. "The LORD appeared to us in the past, saying: 'I have loved you with an everlasting love; I have drawn you with loving- kindness. I will build you up _____ and you will be rebuilt, O Virgin Israel. _____ you will take up your tambourines and go out to dance with the joyful. _____ you will plant vineyards on the hills of Samaria; the farmers will plant them and enjoy their fruit.'"

Fill in the blanks to Jeremiah 33:12. "This is what the LORD Almighty says: 'In this place, _____ and without people or animals—in all its towns there will _____ be pastures for shepherds to rest their flocks.'"

Do you recall the Scripture verse of Week 1, Day 1? It was Jeremiah 33:10. Glance back to that verse. Do you remember how we compared ourselves spiritually to the way Jerusalem was physically to the returning exiles? The wall, temple, and their homes were nothing but rubble. Our spiritual life resembled "rubble" when we returned to our intimate relationship with our heavenly Father.

Since being in the Word over the past five-and-a-half weeks, do you see less rubble and a little more resemblance of normalcy personally? If so, in what ways?

Child, God is doing the "again" in your very life! He hasn't passed you by. He hasn't disqualified you from serving Him. This is how He shows His mercy and compassion. Where we thought there was just emptiness and no hope for anything good in us, God promises to fill us again. As we choose to empty ourselves of worldly passions, He delightfully chooses to fill us with His passions. This He will do for us.

According to the following verses what will God give us again?

Jeremiah 33:6-9

Isaiah 61:7

Zechariah 1:17

Your time of healing has come. Your time of restoration is here. Your time of being comforted is upon you. Your time of rejoicing is forever. Your time of joy is everlasting. Your time of peace and security is not lost. The prosperity of your soul is just beginning. Your God is on your side and He is forever for you.

Let's pray:

For our prayer today let's pray a portion of Psalm 71. Dear heavenly Father, "as for me, I will always have hope; I will praise you more and more. My mouth will tell of your righteousness, of your salvation all day long, though I know not its measure. I will come and proclaim your mighty acts, O Sovereign LORD; I will proclaim your righteousness, yours alone. Since my youth, O God, you have taught me, and to this day I declare your marvelous deeds. Even when I am old and gray, do not forsake me, O God, till I declare your power to the next generation, your might to all who are to come. Your righteousness reaches to the skies, O God, you who have done great things. Who, O God, is like you? Though you have made me see troubles, many and bitter, you will restore my life again; from the depths of the earth you will again bring me up. You will increase my honor and comfort me once again." (Psalm 71: 14–21)In Jesus' name I pray, amen.

Week 6 — What Will I Do?

Day 4 — Free

Today's Scripture:

So if the Son sets you free,
you will be free indeed.

—John 8:36

Yesterday's study brought up the subject of doubt. To doubt is completely normal and rational. Insecurity in oneself is something most everyone battles. For those of us who have undergone self-inflicting wounds, our doubts concerning our worth and value have tripled. So many questions arise. And honestly, it seems no one has a solid enough answer. Questions like:

What if I go back into captivity?

What if I mess up again?

What if I just can't help myself?

What if I don't like my new life at home again?

What if I don't resist temptation again?

What if my struggles never go away?

 What question(s) do you have that seems as if no one can answer?

Child, I am convinced that your toughest battles are behind you. You have made it through some of the fiercest challenges known to Christianity. Being prone to wander away from your Shepherd doesn't mean you will. A Christian isn't lacking in sin, he just doesn't continue in sin. Paul informs us in Galatians 5:1 "It is for freedom that Christ has set us free. Stand firm, then, and do not let yourselves be burdened again by a yoke of slavery." Where you are today and the fact that you have deliberately chosen to participate in this timely Bible study, I believe, means God has set you free. Please read the John 8:36.

 What has God specifically set you free from?

I want you to see John 8:36 in the Amplified Bible. It says, "So if the Son liberates you [makes you free men], then you are really *and* unquestionably free." Period! No more "what if" questions! You are completely free, child! Free from doubting. Free from fear of others. Free from haunting past failures. Free from habitual sin. Free from condemnation. Just plain and simply free.

So, what's a free man or woman to do with all this freedom? Well, you do have a responsibility, actually.

For the remainder of today's study we are going to glimpse into the lives of two radical followers of God whom we can relate to in the area of leaving home and returning. Our first glimpse is in the Old Testament with King David. God called David "a man after God's own heart" (1 Samuel 13:14) even before David was anointed king. He was proclaimed king at the age of 30 and reigned 40 years. David was God's man for leading God's people through wars and battles. During one particular time of war, King David chose not to go with his men. This is when the downfall began. You can read of the account in 2 Samuel 11:1-17, 26-27. Summarize King David's relationship with Bathsheba.

King David's sin was eventually exposed when the prophet Samuel confronted him. Then, in his brokenness, the king acknowledged his sin and turned his heart back to God. His repentance was penned when he revealed his raw emotions becoming transparent for generations to generations to view in Psalm 51. Please read Psalm 51:7-15.

 What responsibility did King David commit to (verse 13)?

Who better to teach others about the agony of sin than the one who experienced it? Who better to teach sinners about the grace of God than the one who received it? You, too, repentant one, God will use to reach others as you become transparent. No need to reveal the details, sin is sin. King David generalized his sin in Psalm 51 in such a practical way that any one of us can identify.

Our second glimpse comes from the powerhouse apostle Peter. Peter was a fisherman before Jesus called him to "catch men" and to follow Him (Luke 5:10b). One of the first miracles Peter witnessed Jesus perform was the healing of his mother-in-law. Over the course of Jesus' three years of ministry, Peter witnessed numerous miracles, including the feeding of the 5,000, Jesus calming a storm, and Jesus walking on water. Peter was also one of three disciples invited to witness the transfiguration of Jesus on the Mount of Olives. It was Peter who confessed Jesus to be God. As the disciples were with Jesus celebrating the Passover (known as the Last Supper), Jesus made known a startling truth that Peter would deny him three times by the next morning. Please read Luke 22:31-34.

 Whom did God allow to sift Peter?

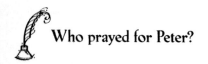

Who prayed for Peter?

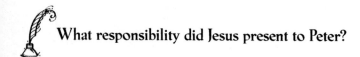

What responsibility did Jesus present to Peter?

Jesus believed Peter needed the sifting and that he would come through it. Jesus also knew you would too. He has been praying for you. Your faith has not failed. It has been put to the test just as Peter's was, and is now stronger than if the test had never occurred.

Did Peter strengthen his brothers? You betcha! Acts Chapters 2—4 records the powerhouse apostle proclaiming Jesus as the Christ and winning soul after soul to the Kingdom of God.

Some may say your testimony is ruined. Some may be in agreement with Satan hoping you will never speak up about your repentance and restoration. Some may stand in judgment over you. Some may never understand you. Some may never embrace you. The truth of the matter is this…God says, "You, then, why do you judge your brother or sister? Or why do you treat them with contempt? For we will all stand before God's judgment seat. It is written, 'As surely as I live,' says the Lord, 'every knee will bow before me; every tongue will confess to God.' So then, each of us will give an account of himself to God" (Romans 14:10-12).

One way or another our knees will be bent in submission to the lordship of Jesus Christ. May we be one who chooses to bow our knees before God everyday of our lives and not wait until Judgment Day.

Let's pray:

Dear heavenly Father, Your Son has set me free. I am no longer bound by chains of my past, but free to bow my knee before You and to confess with my mouth You are Lord indeed. In Jesus' name I pray, amen.

Week 6 — What Will I Do?

Day 5 — Everything We Need

God is so gracious, so faithful. He never changes. His goodness boggles the mind. His ways are higher than ours. His mercy is new every morning. He is beautiful. He is lovely. He is King.

What attributes of God come to your mind today?

Today's Scripture:

His divine power has given us everything we need for a godly life through our knowledge of him who called us by his own glory and goodness.

—2 Peter 1:3

Thanks for hanging in here with me to the completion of *Back From Captivity.* All of our stories are unique, and yet our God unifies us by speaking truths over our lives. I would love to hear your story. I would love to hear you testify of your Redeemer, Rescuer, and Savior. Yours and my story has not ended. There is still more God wants to reveal to us and do for us. This last day of Bible study is the beginning of your future with Him. The King of kings proclaims, "'I am the Alpha and the Omega,' says the Lord God, 'who is, and who was, and who is to come, the Almighty'" (Revelation 1:8). He is with you in your present. He is with you in your past. He is with you in your future. To Him be the glory both now and forevermore.

On my travels back home from a writer's conference, I had a few hours to wait in the airport before I caught my next flight. Since it was close to dinner time, food was definitely on my mind. I headed for the restaurants and found a variety to choose from. Did I want a pretzel? Submarine sandwich? Pizza? Chocolate? Coffee? Snack foods? Nothing sounded just right. Plus, everything was outrageously priced. I decided to go back to my gate and contemplate what I would indulge my taste buds in. As I sat, I realized what I really wanted was something from home—something good for me and something not, "fast food." As I propped my feet up on my carry-on luggage, I remembered something. My carry-on was full of food. Foods that I had bought that were actually good for me. I felt so silly because I had been literally rolling the food behind me in the luggage the whole time I was viewing the different restaurant choices. I had just come from a conference where I was able to cook my own meals, so I brought with me the leftover food. I opened my bag and indulged on my food that I had already purchased.

Isn't that just like us spiritually? God has given us everything we need pertaining to life, but if we don't utilize it, we feel dissatisfied.

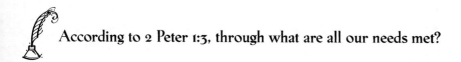 According to 2 Peter 1:3, through what are all our needs met?

 From these Scriptures, write what we are given.

Matthew 7:11

Ephesians 1:3

Philippians 4:19

We truly possess everything we could possibly ever need! Just ask Him, child, for whatever you need! Don't be fooled by the tempting options that appear to be satisfying. Don't be fooled to believe you have to have what the world indulges in. Don't be fooled to think you deserve it. Don't be fooled into paying more than it costs. Don't be fooled into the deception that you need it. Don't be fooled to think it isn't going to hurt anyone. As God's child you have everything you could ever want or need tucked away in a secret place within you. It has already been bought and paid for by the precious blood of the Lamb, Jesus Christ.

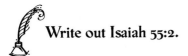 Write out Isaiah 55:2.

Welcome home, child. You are back from captivity. The seductions and temptations of this world have nothing compared to the riches of the Kingdom of God. Enjoy! Be full! Walk straight and tall out of the spiritual intensive care. Child, you are ready! You are indeed a strong, healthy, godly man/ woman. "Arise, shine, for your light has come, and the glory of the LORD rises upon you" (Isaiah 60:1).

Let's pray:

Dear heavenly Father, It's good to be home. It's good to be near You again. It's good to be strong and healthy. I trust You with my life. I pray You will trust me with Yours. I love You. In Jesus' name I pray, Amen.

NOTE TO
Leaders

Visit www.randallhouse.com and receive a free Leader's Guide for *Back From Captivity*. Discover tools to aid you in leading your church or small study group through a six-week journey that gives anyone seeking to restore a relationship with Christ the answers to follow the rebuilding of that most important connection in life.

To order additional copies of *Back From Captivity* call **1-800-877-7030** or log onto www.randallhouse.com. Quantity discount for 24 or more copies at $8.99 each.

ALSO AVAILABLE FROM
Jennifer Johnson

Royal by Blood
ISBN 9780892655700
$10.99

Royal By Blood is a six-week study exploring the role of royalty as well as the role of servant the believer is called to fulfill in God's family. Each week the focus will be taken from the passage in 1Timothy where Paul instructs Timothy to set an example for others to follow. The reader will learn how to relate to God, family, and friends based on the value God places on His creation. Most importantly, each reader should take away a greater personal value realizing God calls a believer an heir to His royal kingdom.

The topics discussed in the study include:

- Eternity in Our Heart
- Gracious Speech
- Living Life with a Right Perspective
- Abounding with Love
- In Increased Faith
- Being Pure

Royal By Blood would be an ideal study for college students who hold Bible studies in the dorm or with a Christian organization on campus. Teens who meet in discipleship classes, neighborhood Bible studies, or with accountability groups would find this study to be very helpful in building stronger relationships.

Order of 24 or more copies will have a quantity discount - $8.99 each

1-800-877-7030
www.randallhouse.com

Notes

Notes

Notes

CPSIA information can be obtained at www.ICGtesting.com
Printed in the USA
LVOW111316290113

317721LV00005B/49/P